KU-168-208

Girl Up Zimbabwe Ambassador, Global University Outreach Manager at One Young World and founder of Empowered by Vee, Vee Kativhu is an education activist and empowerment YouTuber, spreading her message of education, equal access and opportunity, and empowerment to a global audience of over 300,000. At the age of twenty-three, Vee had been named a Diana Award Recipient, LinkedIn Changemaker, United Kingdom Rare Rising Star, United World Schools Ambassador, Social Mobility Foundation Ambassador and a recipient of the Vice Chancellor's Diversity Champion Award. Vee's empowering journey of education, attaining a Bachelor's degree in History from Oxford University and a Master's degree in International Education Policy from Harvard, has earned her praise from the likes of Prince Harry and Meghan Markle as well as features in *The Times* and *The Guardian*.

1 3 5 7 9 8 6 4 2

Square Peg, an imprint of Vintage, One Embassy Gardens,
Nine Elms, London SW11 7AY

Square Peg is part of the Penguin Random House group
of companies whose addresses can be found at: global.
penguinrandomhouse.com

Penguin
Random House
UK

Text copyright © Varaidzo Kativhu 2021

Varaidzo Kativhu has asserted her right to be identified as
the author of this Work in accordance with the Copyright,
Designs and Patents Act 1988

First published by Square Peg in 2021

Penguin.co.uk/vintage

A CIP catalogue record for this book is available from
the British Library

ISBN 9781529110456

Typeset and designed by Nikki Ellis

Cover design by Kishan Rajani

Printed and bound in Great Britain by Clays Ltd, Elcograf S.p.A.

The authorised representative in the EEA is Penguin Random
House Ireland, Morrison Chambers, 32 Nassau Street, Dublin
D02 YH68

Penguin Random House is committed to a sustainable future for
our business, our readers and our planet. This book is made from
Forest Stewardship Council® certified paper.

DEDICATED TO MY BEAUTIFUL MOTHER,
LOVENESS AND MY GUARDIAN ANGEL,
MY FATHER, BRIGHTON KATIVHU.

Contents

A Note from Vee

Throughout this book, the topic of self-empowerment is referenced constantly. Sometimes I forget I need to define the term because it looks different for everyone. For me, self-empowerment is the truest form of self-love. It is the act of ensuring, to the best of your ability, that you are leading a life where you feel in control, in charge of your happiness and the author of your own narrative. It is the act of pursuing your dreams, peace, and everything in between.

Self-empowerment can come in different shapes and sizes: for some people it can be the act of attending a gender pay gap protest, while for others it can be the art of learning to say no and setting better boundaries. The beauty of self-empowerment is that it revolves around the individual and their needs and desires. It centres on you and it's something that comes from within. It shouldn't be controlled by anyone else. For me, self-empowerment has now become a lifestyle. I explore all possibilities, take risks, and always bet on myself.

My deepest and truest form of self-empowerment comes from education, experiences, and opportunities. My education has given me a voice and helped me find my true passion: helping others. It's granted me access to learn about the lives of people around the world and the skills and tools I need to help fight for educational equality for other young women across the globe. My self-empowerment journey has led me down a path of curiosity and armed me with the most powerful tool of all: knowledge. Something that nobody can ever take away from me.

Self-empowerment hasn't always been easy for me, and up until now, it's safe to say my life has been a rollercoaster, full of bumps, twists, and many turns. I figured, whilst I'm still young and have the time, I should write down my thoughts and document the events that have occurred in my life so far, in the hope that my story might encourage others to pursue their own dreams and ambitions. I decided to share my journey a few years ago, after I realised my story carries not only power, but acts as a source of hope and encouragement for others. I wanted to tell my own story because the narratives associated with young people are so often shaped or moulded in a discouraging or unrepresentative light. We're stereotyped and placed in boxes that don't show what we *really* stand for and, as a consequence, sweeping generalisations about our identities are made.

My purpose in writing this book is not to showcase myself, rather it is the recognition that I have struggled; however in that struggle, I have learned many lessons that have helped me overcome the moments of hardship that I never thought I would. My hope is that by sharing my journey, it may be helpful or beneficial to others in similar or somewhat relatable situations. The eleven chapters in this book will cover topics such as how to find your purpose, how to deal with rejection and imposter syndrome, and how to set life goals and lean on others for support. It will cover practical things like how to handle your money, build more empowering relationships and find growth in experiences you may hate. These chapters will also delve more deeply into my own life, some of the difficulties I have faced and how I took those lemons and made them into (delicious) lemonade. I want this book to speak to young people and those who come from a similar background to myself, but I also hope that it'll be used for self-reflection, motivation, and empowerment by many others. I recognise that my story isn't entirely unique, but that's why I'm eager to share it. I know many of you reading this will relate and I hope that this will shine a light on the real lives that so many of us lead, but don't often see written about. Those of us who come from working-class, single-parent households. Those of us who have migrated to new countries and learned new languages. Those of us for whom the journey has not been easy – whether due to lack of finances, resources, opportunities or, often, love. My book represents the many, *not* the few. I want everyone who reads this to close the final chapter and no longer feel alone. I want those who read this to encourage, support, and empower themselves and others around them.

Since embarking on my journey of self-empowerment and putting myself out there on the internet, I've learned a lot about myself. I've begun to understand my emotions more deeply and, as a result, adapted and improved my methods of coping. Before this I was guilty of self-indulging in my negative emotions, questioning why bad things happened to me. I'd wear my emotions – anger, self-pity, sadness – on my sleeve. Rather than *feeling* sad, I would *become* sad. By this, I mean I would *talk* sad, *think* sad, *walk* sad, *act* sad . . . you get the gist. Rather than momentarily allowing the emotion to pass, I allowed the feeling to become permanent and to consume me. I'd question things for days on end, wondering how bad things could happen to good people, why God hadn't given me a chance to be happy when I was just an innocent child trying to survive life. I felt almost constantly demoralised, and despite physically having my mother and sister in my life, I still felt alone and abandoned with my thoughts.

When I discovered the power of positive thinking, my mindset completely changed. I began to speak things into existence. I began dressing how I wanted to be addressed – though I like to use this term both lightly and cautiously. When I say this, what I mean is I began to go through life the way I wanted the world to see me. I presented myself in the way that I wanted to be seen and treated. I wanted the world to take me seriously, to have faith in me and my abilities, so I began behaving accordingly.

Firstly, I decided what I wanted to do:

1. To make history
2. To create global change for girls' education
3. To make an impact on the lives of others
4. To leave my mark on the world

Eager to achieve these goals, I started learning about the art of valuing *my* time; not feeling guilty for prioritising the things that mattered to me before looking after everyone else. I then turned my attention to cutting out those 'bad eggs' – the people who made me doubt myself, the ones who did not want to see me grow. I realised that you cannot change your life if the systems around you do not change, and having people with a negative mindset was only going to bring me back to that space. I then began working on mastering my talents, and one of those was the art of 'speaking'. I knew that if I wanted to be heard, I needed to say something worth hearing. As a young child, I had loved making speeches in front of my family, reading aloud in class, and performing with my friends. My teachers used to call me either 'smiler' or 'speaker' because, as you can guess, I smiled and spoke a lot. Despite sometimes getting in trouble for speaking too much in class, every time that I spoke, people always wanted more. They said my voice had a way of drawing them in and my passion left them feeling inspired, no matter the subject.

I noticed this more once I became an ambassador for the Social Mobility Foundation, a charity that helps students from underrepresented and 'underprivileged' backgrounds. The SMF are so incredibly helpful to students who are bright but don't have the means or support to access the school of their dreams. The more students I was required to mentor, help, and support, the more confident I became. Not only did I see students grow in their abilities, I saw this in myself too. Since that moment of realising the impact I had on others, there was absolutely no way that I could stand up and tell these students, younger than myself, to believe in *themselves* when *I* doubted *me*. Thus, my journey to self-empowerment was fuelled by the empowerment of others. I began speaking to myself in the same way I spoke to my mentees and removed negativity from my vocabulary. You see, we don't often realise this but we're a million times kinder to others than we are to ourselves. We speak to ourselves or about ourselves in ways that we would *never* dream of speaking to or about our friends, family or even strangers. Whenever I felt like I was being harsh on myself, I would look in the mirror and simply tell myself to be kinder. I'd recite a stream of affirmative words, a task that was not and will *never* be comfortable, but is absolutely necessary. The more I did it, the easier it became.

> *My journey to self-empowerment began with the empowerment of others. I began speaking to myself in the same way I spoke to my mentees and removed negativity from my vocabulary.*

You see, you are going to be you for the rest of your life, so it's not just about *living* with yourself, it's also about *loving* yourself. Don't get me wrong, these things are definitely easier said than done but I promise, realising how amazing and worthy you are is the first (and most important) step to self-empowerment. So, next time you're beating yourself down, ask yourself . . .

- Is this productive?
- Is this helping me?
- Is this giving me more confidence or adding to my empowerment journey?
- Would I speak to a stranger like this?

If the answers are no, then please STOP. What you need to remember, when it comes to self-empowerment, is that YOU are living YOUR life for YOU. Everything happens for a reason and the only timing you need to focus on is your own. This might sound simple to remember theoretically but practically? Not so much. It might take you five years to achieve what your friends have done in two, but that's okay! Before starting my undergrad, I had to take an extra year out to complete a foundation year. Lots of people around me tried to dissuade me. I was told I was 'wasting my time', that I'd be 'behind my peers' and that it was a 'risky move for my future' because foundation years weren't seen in a positive light at the time. I still decided to follow my heart and to ignore the (unwanted) opinions I was receiving. Everyone's journey is different; yours might just take a little longer. For me, that foundation year became the best decision I've made in my life so far. I could not have written a better outcome from it even if I had tried.

My foundation year allowed me to spend an extra year at Oxford University before beginning my undergraduate degree and ultimately led me to finding social media, creating my channel and to now: writing this book! Taking an extra year out of university literally changed the course of my life and it was all because I trusted my gut and followed my own timeline. That trust came from deep within, from a place of desire, a desire to have control over my own life and not live for others. One of my favourite affirmation mantras is that 'I am good enough and 100 per cent deserve to achieve the things I truly want in this life.' Once I had engrained this philosophy into my mind, I saw everything differently. Every bad situation turned into an opportunity and every glass I saw previously as half-empty became half-full. With self-worth now a key part my being I felt unstoppable, and I truly hope that once you've finished reading this book, you'll feel the same.

Vee x

Finding Your Purpose

HOW TO EMPOWER YOURSELF IN YOUR WORK AND EDUCATION

How did you find your purpose?

This is a question I am asked on a regular basis, and I respond the same way each time.

'It found me.'

It's not the most helpful of answers but it's my truth. I often follow up their question by asking four of my own:

1. What issues in the world keep you awake at night?
2. What would you not mind fighting for/working on for the rest of your life?
3. What makes you feel alive? Passionate? Angry? Happy?
4. What motivates you to get up and go every day?

Essentially, what I'm asking is, what is the 'thing' that makes them feel. Whatever that is, that's their purpose. My mission to empower, educate and fight for those whose voices are so often silenced has become my calling because I have witnessed first-hand in my family the lifetime damage that being silenced, having a lack of choice and education can do to women and I never want another young girl to experience that, hence my unwavering passion to get up every day and do what I can to help fight that cause. So, how do you find this 'thing' inside you? Think about debates you find difficult to leave, the problem you can't stop pondering over or the projects you find yourself volunteering to help with. What world issue, cause, or task would you give anything to be a part of changing? Whatever *that* is, that's your *thing*; explore it further.

How the past informed my purpose

An example of the way my internal motivation helps me shape my purpose is with my country of birth, Zimbabwe. I care so deeply about seeing it transform to stability that I find myself pursuing this cause on a regular basis and shaping my life around it. For this to make sense, I need to share my story properly by taking you back to the beginning, and for that we need to get personal.

I was born and raised in Zimbabwe, a place that I so deeply love and feel connected to. Zimbabwe is one of the most beautiful countries in the world, hidden at the southern end of the African continent. It was in this bright, beautiful and complex country that baby Varaidzo was born in April of 1998.

My name, Varaidzo, translated into English means 'to soothe or to entertain: Ku Varaidza'. My family laugh at the irony, saying I have gone on to become the embodiment of my name. I agree with them, I believe my desire to help other people has always been with me. It stems from events that have occurred in my childhood and my past. I suppose the idea here is that, because I had experienced pain and personal suffering in my childhood, I wanted to help alleviate it in other people.

Although Zimbabwe is a country of pride, filled with culture and a deep history, it's also a country that carries a lot of pain and is still healing from the tragedy that was inflicted upon it. Our economy is still to recover, and our politics are yet to be free from corruption. I hope to see the rebuilding of Zimbabwe happen in my generation's lifetime, to see young people come together to help forge a better future by acknowledging our country's past, while actively trying to dismantle its remnants. I have hope that change will come as there are so many grassroots organisations working endlessly to empower young people to take action, educate themselves, and encourage others to do the same. In the future, I hope to go back to Zimbabwe and work alongside educators to help reform and shape education policy to ensure that we have young people, especially girls, receiving a free, safe, and uncompromised education. I want to see the gender gap, in all sectors, bridged so that girls are given access to the same opportunities as boys. I want to see child marriage made an illegal act punishable by imprisonment and girls given full protection and support against this. I want to see equity within the labour workforce: many girls are allowed to enter schools and get an education, but once they leave, they are still not allowed to get jobs or climb the financial ladder. I want to see change in the way that society views the value of the female gender and for them to be considered first-class citizens in the same way men are. In the next ten years, it would be incredible to see a young woman running for office and getting elected. Giving women a seat at the table, the same way men are, will truly change the prosperity of Zimbabwe and propel us into a new space of much needed change.

In the future, I hope to go back to Zimbabwe and work alongside educators to help reform and shape education policy to ensure that we have young people, especially girls, receiving a free, safe, and uncompromised education.

At the time that I was born, my family lived a happy life: my mum, dad and their two girls, my sister Fadziee and me. My father worked as a pharmacist and was highly regarded in his community as he was known as the man with the answers, the man with the plan. He enjoyed arts and crafts on the side and spent his days creating custom-made calendars that he would pass around to family members and friends.

He loved to travel and was a man with a deep curiosity about the world and his place in it. From what my mother told me, he questioned many things around him and was deeply – as she loves to remind us – in love with his wife, her. But their happiness was short-lived, for the wonderful man I have heard so much about passed away eight days after my second birthday in the year 2000. Despite me not truly knowing him, to this day I still mourn him.

There is always this feeling, a constant longing and recognition that something is missing; his love, guidance and protection, despite never truly having it. And these emotions make me wonder, what is better: to have had someone and then lost them, or not to have ever had them at all? Because the feeling of never actually knowing him hurts more than words can describe. It leaves many questions unanswered for me, almost as if a part of my identity disappeared before I got the chance to discover it.

I know we are only genetic products of our parents, and that the rest – learning their mannerisms, values and beliefs – is a matter of nurture. However, I wanted to witness first hand if what my family have been saying is true: that I look like him, speak like him, squint my eyes when reading in a similar fashion to him, and have a burning curiosity for the world like him. They tell me he loved to travel and planned to take his family travelling in the future once my sister and I were old enough to remember it. According to my mum and the rest of my extended family, I was close to my father and despite being only two years old, was aware of his presence and was less agitated around him. I, of course, have no recollection of these memories, however I have heard them so often that these memories now feel like my own.

My mum says that I was the baby that was given more independence. The one left to experiment and play in the mud freely. My sister, on the other hand, prefered the gentler and less messy side of life, she always kept her clothes clean and played inside. Where I was eager to stop breastfeeding, she had fought to stay on; where I learned how to walk before my time, she had preferred to be carried. They say Fadziee took after my mum and that I was my father's twin. Thus, when his death arrived, perhaps two-year-old Vee was more aware of his loss than I give credit for.

My mum told me that at the funeral, I cried for her to let me kiss him so that I could wake him up. Apparently, it was a game we used to play. He would pretend to sleep and only wake up when I had kissed him. She says that even at that young age, I had become known for trying to heal family members with a kiss whenever they were unwell or displaying pain. She said that I was also notorious for standing in between the other babies I played with to try and stop them from fighting. She noted how whenever I failed to make people smile or stop crying , I would become quiet or sad and sit in a corner alone. As such, my behaviour at the funeral did not come as a shock to anyone who knew my character. As I've gotten older I am realising that my sadness as a child was not about the other person not getting better or waking up, but the realisation that I was powerless, that I could not physically or emotionally heal everyone by a magic kiss or smile. Whatever it was that existed within me, that deep desire to always help grew into the driving force for the things I do and the life I lead today as an adult.

After my father's death, my mother had to unfortunately relocate to England to make ends meet, start afresh and keep us safe. My sister and I had to stay in Zimbabwe until we could join her once she had saved enough to fly us over. In that time, four years to be precise, my sister and I were separated, living from auntie to uncle depending on who could afford to have us that month. (My grandma had fourteen children so we really did move around every few months). This was by far the hardest time of my life. For a long time, I felt alone and abandoned. I felt as though God had punished me for a crime I didn't commit. I am sure that the adults around us had the intentions to protect us, but they failed. Many incidents of emotional, physical and sexual abuse occurred that should never have. I found myself constantly feeling on edge, never knowing when the next bad thing would happen. I began having regular nightmares and became jumpy from things such as being pranked with rubber snakes or having buckets of cold water thrown over me while I slept. I also remember feeling guilty and like a burden for the people I was living with. It felt like there was never any room for me. I missed my family, my deceased father, my absent mother and my separated sister, a family I'd not had the chance to know.

Although I was now only about four or five years old, I remember feeling fed up and sad enough that one day I decided to run away. I apparently knew my way from one family member's home to the other as they all lived within close proximity to one another, so I grabbed a few items and made my way. This was the house where my sister was staying and I had not seen her in a long time and desperately wanted to be there too. I remember arriving and seeing her through the kitchen window which faced the entrance gate, and feeling pure joy.

I am forever grateful to my auntie for taking me in that day and giving me something I had not had up until that point: stability. It was the first time I felt I had a family and some form of structure. Her two children became the siblings I'd always wished for and from that day, we were raised as a four. To this day we are still incredibly close and still operate as siblings not cousins. I respected my uncle, their dad, so much, he was one of the kindest men I've ever known. My relationship with my uncle is the first memory of a father figure that I really have. He treated all four of us equally and unless someone knew, people could never guess who his biological children were versus his nieces. I have to be clear that despite this newfound stability and family unit, there was still a lot of pain endured through neglect, more emotional trauma and other events I cannot yet bring myself to discuss and still feel the impact of now. However, those moments of sadness were definitely outweighed by the goodness of my uncle. He became my sister and I's safe space and without him I am not sure I would have mentally survived that time in my life.

We began attending school, my uncle would take us all and pick us up. We would play, travel around Zimbabwe and create memories. The love I experienced from my uncle will live in my heart forever and his bright light during a dark part of my life saved me as a child. He sadly passed away a year after I had moved to England, a heartbreak that will stay with me forever.

For a long time, after coming to England and being reunited with my mum, I felt guilty for having negative thoughts about my time without her in Zimbabwe. I felt indebted to the people who had taken me in and wished I could alter some of the feelings of sadness that I had experienced to show my gratitude for their kindness, but it was impossible. I remember my mum bursting into tears once my sister and I had told her about the things that had taken place.

I want to highlight that sadly this type of story isn't unique. It is a common one among so many of my friends and cousins who also had parents migrate to the United Kingdom during this time. I have had endless conversations with them about their feelings and experiences and they all share the same sentiments. All of us, it seems, are fighting between the same emotions; simultaneously feeling deep sadness but also immense gratitude to those who took us in. There are many reasons why our parents made the move: to escape political violence, poverty, dictatorships, and a general lack of opportunity. Whatever the reasons, many of us were left alone and those are moments when things like abuse, neglect and manipulation occur, and it is extremely sad because children should be protected at all costs. It hurts my heart that this type of childhood is one that many can relate to. However, it brings me joy to see that those who have endured the same experiences are now prospering, processing some of those events and on journeys of healing.

I am a firm believer in acknowledging errors and bad moments of judgement in order to move on in a healthy and productive manner.

I, for one, am still figuring it out and will continue working on my own growth and journey of healing. I do want to make it clear that I still have respect for the people who looked after us while my mum was away. They opened up their hearts and homes to us in our time of need and for that, I will forever be grateful. However, it would be dishonest to ignore the mistakes that did occur and I am a firm believer in acknowledging errors and bad moments of judgement in order to move on in a healthy and productive manner. I just wanted to share what a difficult time it was for me following my father's death and being separated from my mum and sister, to help you understand me better.

So, after four years when the time finally came to join our mother in England, you can imagine my excitement. A fresh chapter was beginning, I quickly rebonded with my mum and began our new lives in Birmingham. I attended a local primary school where I began learning English and made my first set of friends. These girls are still some of my closest friends to this day and I truly appreciate their patience in helping me speak English, and navigate a new culture; introducing me to snow and the joys of 'fish and chips'. It did not take me long to learn English as I picked up things like languages quite quickly. I soon became one of the fastest readers in my class – if not *the* fastest. The stories I read were magical and left me feeling like I could do and be anything. I engrossed myself in each book and did not put it down until it was finished. The books helped me escape the sad thoughts that I would often have about the life I had lived back in Zimbabwe – for me, reading felt therapeutic and soothing. In my spare time I would try and help the slower readers in my class by teaching them my little techniques. I pretended to be characters from the books I read, or I imagined the scenes of the book as a movie in my head, or my favourite strategy was reading out loud and acting out the scenes. My teacher would tell me off for this, calling my behaviour 'disruptive' and writing in my school reports that I would benefit from being a little quieter. But when my friends thanked me in the playground for helping them, I'd feel so fulfilled and content that telling off from the teacher would be worth it. I would continuously find myself diving into any challenge that would help me help my classmates. I sought out voluntary activities in school such as joining the 'Friendship Stop': a place where we, as primary school students, could help each other with issues such as making friends or speaking about our worries or bad things going on at home. I had become extremely in tune with my empathy and was giving advice to my peers from an early age.

I AM NOT SURE IF MY TRAUMA FROM ZIMBABWE HAD ANYTHING TO DO WITH IT BUT EITHER WAY I ALWAYS FOUND MYSELF DRAWN TO ALLEVIATING THE DISTRESS OF OTHERS AROUND ME.

How outrage fuelled my purpose

Now in my adult life the desire to help has evolved specifically into the realm of education where I take pride in assisting young people in getting access to education. My favourite moments are when I can guide people to realise their full potential and discover their self-worth. To see that they are more than the negative labels and stereotypes that society tries to place on them. With hindsight, I do now see how this was fuelled by my childhood. I hated that people pre-judged me or placed me in a box simply because I physically did not have my parents around me. I was therefore considered by our cultural standards a 'nherera' (which. translates directly to orphan: and used to mean a Zimbabwean child without a FATHER). I hated the negative connotations attached to the term 'nherera', which labelled me in the light of pity before people got to know me.

As I made my way through my teenage years, I would always battle with my friends during sixth form because they always put themselves down. They thought that because we were from less privileged backgrounds, we couldn't dream big. In their defence, we were the few Black and brown students at my sixth form and we felt it. We were also slightly different from everyone else in that we rarely ate in the school canteen because it was too expensive, and instead would put our money together to get meal deals at our local Chicken Hut. Most of our classmates did not have to work, while we would juggle our A-Levels and part-time jobs. I will always remember finishing class, running to the toilets to change into my McDonald's uniform and doing my homework on the bus ride to work. I was always exhausted but knew that I could not ask my mum for money as she was just about making ends meet for herself and our family, therefore I had to take on more hours to sustain myself. One day my manager shouted at me for reading

Hamlet in preparation for my exam the next day, instead of interacting with my co-workers during my work break. I cried about that when I got home but grew thick skin because I knew that book, that exam and my dreams were my ticket to having choices and making the life I wanted for myself. I wanted more than what I had seen and knew that pursuing my education was the only way that I could make my voice heard. My friends also knew this and thus in our spare time, when not working our jobs, we would study day and night. We would gather at one person's house, order takeaway and go over our material until we knew it inside out.

WE WERE INCREDIBLY HARD WORKING, BUT JUST HAD SOCIAL BARRIERS THAT MEANT WE ALWAYS FELT BEHIND OUR PEERS, NO MATTER HOW HARD WE TRIED.

Now I need to make it explicitly clear that there is nothing wrong with working at McDonalds. I did so for over a year and it was truly the most enriching experience that left me with more life skills than I could ever imagine. McDonalds taught me the art of problem-solving – dealing with angry customers means thinking on your feet 24/7 to ensure their problem is fixed. Doing this over and over again taught me how to read people, how to de-escalate situations and how to manage high-stress environments. Despite the lifelong skills I gained, I wish I'd been able to spend more time studying than working at that age.

What I did realise while sixteen and working at McDonalds was that many people from areas like mine were not receiving the same opportunities as students from more privileged backgrounds. My friends and I used to see our peers learning how to drive, the lessons paid for by their parents, and receiving their first cars by the age of eighteen, while other young people were working almost full-time hours to save for their bus passes. My peers, who now had cars, could access better work experiences because they could make regular commutes to farther places. They could easily go home in between study breaks; something that they told me improved their mental health during exam season. They said having cars, no jobs and financial freedom enhanced their learning experience because they were less stressed. They shared how when they fell behind in classes their parents would pay for tutors to give them private help at home to catch up. They would buy the expensive class textbooks and use them in the comfort of their home and learn at their own pace. Luxuries that my friends and I did not have. These concepts of financial and social inequality became even more apparent when I became a member of the Social Mobility Foundation and began my Foundation Year at Oxford. For the first time in my life, I had a glaring face-to-face with the reality that people like myself were actually considered to be 'poor'. Despite having to work throughout my sixth form years and not affording what my peers could, I had always considered myself lucky. Lucky to even have the chance to work, have access to an education and even be able to buy food at lunchtime with my friends. I was aware I was not from a wealthy background

What I did realise while sixteen and working at McDonalds was that many people from areas like mine were not receiving the same opportunities as students from more privileged backgrounds.

but I had never felt poor, not until Oxford. I'd always been aware that we lacked financial and social capital. I noticed that we lacked 'nice' things at sixth form when I saw that my peers could afford more things than I could, but still I never felt poor because my mom had always showed us how to make the little money we did have stretch. However, at the beginning of my time at Oxford I felt poor. I really began to doubt myself and feel out of place. When I looked around the city, I did not see many people who looked or spoke like me and that bothered me a lot and made me question whether someone like me belonged there.

At first, these feelings did not bother me too much. I figured people come from different walks of life. I decided to see the lack of diversity as an opportunity to showcase my strengths and abilities *despite* my background. What *did* bother me however was what happened when I went back home. I specifically remember the first university break we had: I got home and everyone was showering me with praise. They told me I was amazing, inspiring and that I was already helping change the world. I did not, for the life of me, understand why they were saying this. I mean don't get me wrong, I understood Oxford's reputation and the global name that it carried as one of the oldest and most prestigious universities. However, I did not understand why *me* studying *there* was given the same attention and acclaim as if I'd single-handedly found the cure for cancer or ended world hunger. I was told I was 'doing the exceptional' and was 'giving everyone hope'. When I finally realised why they were saying this to me, I was first sad then angry. My friends were in awe because they believed a place at Oxford was something above them. This infuriated me. Why should my being at Oxford give anyone hope? I'd sat in rooms with many of my fellow university students and whilst many of them were really great, they weren't the mythical people that my friends were imagining them to be. They were smart, really smart, but they weren't *the* smartest people to ever walk the earth. It was almost as if my friends and other people thought they were unicorns, rather than who they actually were – students who happened to be studying at a well-known university. But no matter what I said, my friends at home were now under the impression that students at Oxford were better and more deserving of opportunities (like having the chance to possibly lead the country one day) than they were, solely by virtue of the university they attended. My friends saw themselves as 'inferior' and 'less than' for not attending an institution like that, so my being there was truly viewed as a symbol of hope for them and many others in my community.

But no matter what I said, my friends at home were now under the impression that students at Oxford were better and more deserving of opportunities (like having the chance to possibly lead the country one day) than they were, solely by virtue of the university they attended.

IT MADE ME FURIOUS.

What was most infuriating about it was that I knew my friends were incredibly smart, incredibly talented and could run circles around half the Oxford students I knew. They were just as passionate about their subjects and future goals as my Oxford peers. However, due to lack of opportunity and resources they simply didn't get the chance to even enter the race because they did not have access to the arena. 'But Vee, if your friends found it difficult, how did you get into Oxford?' I hear you ask. That is a good question, one that we will get into in our 'Rejection is Redirection' chapter (on page 52), but for now, just know that it wasn't through the conventional route. The external factors that were in the way of my friends and I felt unfair because they were completely out of our control; we had lost the race before it had even begun. Our postcodes, school type, household incomes, race, class and many other things contributed to us falling behind our privileged counterparts without even knowing it. It was from this anger combined with my traumatic childhood that I discovered the cause I wanted to begin campaigning for.

My anger helped me start taking action after identifying the problem and revisiting my own life experiences. I didn't want another young Black student or someone from a lower socioeconomic background to doubt their worth based on that very background. I didn't want them to have their value based on a particular university. At the same time I had no right to tell anyone how they should measure their value, so if a specific university was their dream, I did not want them to give up the process of applying because they thought their background made them inferior. I wanted to help make sure that young people around me felt empowered in what they did, whether it was applying for the most competitive internships, starting a business or working in retail. Whatever their desires were, I needed them to understand that they were within their reach with the help of a few resources along the way. Hearing the way my friends had spoken about their inferiority, a feeling I related to before I had arrived at Oxford, broke my heart. I wanted them to know they could have control of their own narrative and that the world was for the taking, as long as they wanted it.

The first action I took in helping towards the issue of academic self-confidence and tackling imposter syndrome was by becoming an access and outreach ambassador for my favourite charity, The Social Mobility Foundation, and my university. I became a mentor, a university tour guide and a go-to source of advice for applying to higher education programmes. I then launched a YouTube channel where I began campaigning as an education advocate for diversity and access, growing a student community of over 250,000 young people around the world in need of academic empowerment. I then became a ChangeMaker for LinkedIn, was awarded the Rare Rising Star award by members of the UK parliament for my social media advocacy for students, and received a Diversity and Equality Champion award from the Vice Chancellor of Oxford University. We'll dig into how all this happened in later chapters, but essentially, I began to dedicate my time and energy to the causes I cared about. Since embarking on my fight for fair access to education, I've met some of the most inspirational people, made speeches on incredible stages and sat at dinner tables with some incredibly powerful people. Setting up my YouTube channel was my way of rebelling against the systems of inequality I had witnessed.

THE MORE I READ ABOUT THE ADMISSIONS STATS FOR BLACK STUDENTS AT OXFORD, THE MORE I FELT MY PURPOSE CALLING ME. THE ANGRIER I FELT, THE MORE EMPOWERED AND IMPASSIONED I BECAME. ALONG MY JOURNEY I HAVE HAD THE PRIVILEGE OF TOUCHING THE LIVES OF LITERALLY THOUSANDS OF STUDENTS AND AS I HELPED THEM CHANGE THEIR LIVES, THEY WERE IN TURN HELPING ME CHANGE MINE.

How to find opportunities that inform your purpose

Perhaps your purpose does not stem from your past or even from a place of anger or rage. Many people tend to find their purpose by trying multiple things and checking off their list as they go; this is something I have also done. For example, if I find an internship that I'm interested in, I will take it and try it, and at the end of that internship I will weigh up the pros and cons of the experience and decide if I liked it. I have undertaken work experience placements and internships at Channel 4, BBC, ITV, WPP, JP Morgan, a high school, Boots Pharmacy, a restaurant, a car dealership, and a charity in Zimbabwe. Each of these experiences taught me something new and helped me check off the list what I did not want to do, which in turn brought me one step closer to what I actually wanted to do. Gaining experience, whether it's voluntary or paid, will help you learn a lot about yourself, your tolerances, your strengths, and your weaknesses. This is a great way to find what you like because it exposes you to many different roles and helps you discover jobs that you may not have known existed.

One of my former mentees was struggling to choose which path she wanted to pursue; she found it difficult to make decisions and felt fearful that whichever choice she made might be the wrong one. She was torn between taking an internship in media or one in banking. I told her either choice would be okay and that she should stop worrying. She was so young, in her first year of university, and had her whole life ahead of her to figure out what she wanted to do. I told her that the only way she could guarantee not knowing what she wanted to do was by not trying. Not trying things out leads to not having answers, whereas trying at least provides us with insight into how we feel about these industries or job roles. In order for her to know what she really wanted to do, she equally needed to discover what she really did not want to do.

My various work experience placements and internships have helped me learn what kind of environment I would enjoy working in best and what kind of teammate I am. I quickly learned that I prefer fast-paced environments that provide new challenges and that I hate slow-moving tasks that are repetitive. I relish receiving my tasks and going about trying to accomplish them. I hate being micromanaged and realised I am not fond of group projects. I learned that I enjoy practical, hands-on tasks, whereas those that are only computer or desk-based make me want to cry from boredom. I also quickly came to learn that I thrive in collaborative environments – not so much group work, but a space where ideas can be brainstormed together and the project becomes an amalgamation of everyone's thoughts. I like spaces where my voice can be heard, and being given a chance to contribute no matter how junior my position. These internships and work experiences really helped me come into my own as a young person, to understand what mattered most to me, and what I wanted to dedicate my time and energy to.

SO, MY ADVICE FOR THOSE OF YOU WHO DON'T KNOW WHERE TO BEGIN WITH FINDING YOUR PURPOSE OR THE PATH THAT YOU WANT TO PURSUE NOW IS TO GO AND EXPLORE YOUR OPTIONS.

Suggestions on how to begin discovering your purpose

1. Go on LinkedIn and search for job titles you are interested in. Read the job descriptions line for line and make a pros and cons list of the things you like and don't like. Once that list is complete, move on to the next few roles until you feel you have a good amount. Then compare them to find which job role has more pros on its list, or explore the commonalities in your pros lists and begin to narrow down which pros are things you are looking for and which are must-haves in your job. The roles with the most pros are the ones you should explore in further depth first, for example by looking on the company's website for more information on the job, and then applying.

2. Scout out the people who have that role and see what they have to say about it. Reach out to them and ask if you can have a Zoom coffee chat about their role (people are usually flattered that you have taken an interest in what they do and are usually happy to help if asked kindly).

3. Ask around by word-of-mouth and see what your friends or friends of your friends do. Find out if they enjoy their roles, and once again, ask for a fifteen-minute chat to gain some insight.

4. Seek out a careers advisor online or at university. Tell them your interests and current hobbies. They can take this information and suggest some careers to explore.

5. Do some voluntary work for a few weeks at the places you care about, like an animal shelter, charity organisation, local school, etc., and see how you feel afterwards and if it's something you could dedicate longer periods of time to. For example, you could volunteer at your local charity shop, helping them to find new ways of attracting more donations or helping them to build a social media presence to attract more customers. Perhaps you could offer your services to a local animal rescue shelter, helping them look through their data to see the typical places they find animals to rescue. With this data you could help them identify a pattern for the reasons people give their pets away, and why they are left in particular areas. This could help the rescue shelter find a common trend and thus find the animals quicker than they usually do.

6. Draw up a five-year plan. Include where you would like to see yourself in five years' time. Ask yourself about the kind of life you would be living, the kind of friends you would have and the elements of the job that you would do. Doing this exercise helps you realise how much your dreams match up with the things you are currently pursuing.

Now, I know that even with this advice and the resources to begin searching, you might still feel frustrated and nowhere near finding what you'd like to pursue. This feeling is normal and is one that will most likely be present for a while until you become comfortable with the process and idea of not having all of the answers. You will have to understand that this is a journey of discovery. You won't always know what's coming next. You have to envision yourself as an explorer, someone who is searching for hidden treasures and to do so, you must keep an open mind, be willing to look everywhere and, most importantly, not give up. We will talk about this more in our 'Lean on Them' chapter (on page 92), but your knowledge only spans so far, so digging into other people's experiences and getting advice will always help you with understanding various industries and roles better.

Also, being open about your journey and your struggle with finding your purpose gives people a chance to try and help. I recall complaining to my friend that I didn't know how to break into the media industry as, at the time, I wanted to be a presenter and reporter, someone who travels the world finding stories on education – or, the lack thereof, and the consequences of that. I wanted to get in touch with journalists but had no idea how. My friend then came back to me a few weeks later and let me know about a new society that was forming in our university, the Media Society. The society planned to invite various speakers, people who were prominent in the media, to give a talk and the whole event would be organised by members. I immediately applied for a society position and was given the Head of Communications role. This meant that I was now able to go back and forth with the speakers and form relationships and bonds with them. Once the speakers had given their talks, the committee members were able to have drinks and tea with them and this is how I came to get my internships. I remember hosting Jon Snow, a renowned television presenter of Channel 4 News, for our launch event. We had wonderful conversations about his time travelling on the African continent, his groundbreaking interview with Nelson Mandela and various other things. During the conversation, I let him know about my dreams and my struggle with breaking into the industry, and just like that, on the spot, he offered me work experience at Channel 4 News. We swapped contact details, and a few months later I was in London interning with him. Through this internship I met people like Cathy Newman and Ben De Pear. People who gave me incredible advice and

Do not be afraid to ask for help. You never know what someone may be able to do for you on your quest to find your purpose.

helped me understand the industry better. I had such a great time at my mini-internship and worked incredibly hard at the tasks I was given and, after it was over, they invited me back several times for paid work, which felt incredible. My point here is, opportunity often comes in the most unexpected of moments and the most unexpected of times, but when it does, be prepared to take it. My openness in the conversation with Jon Snow led me to finding work experience that I really loved. People are often willing to help when they know how they can. Jon Snow heard my problem and just so happened to be in a position where he could help. The moment he said he could do so, I ensured I followed up through email and acted with promptness to show him I was serious and ready to take the opportunity he had presented to me. So, do not be afraid to ask for help. You never know what someone may be able to do for you on your quest to find your purpose.

What if you have multiple interests or purposes?

Remember that humans are multifaceted beings and you can have multiple interests that all exist side by side. It's okay if your purpose isn't limited to just one thing and if you shift focus every few years. I'm interested in national and higher education for UK students, but I *equally* care about girls' education in low-income countries and want to help reduce the number of girls out of school. At the same time, I care about ending child marriage, homelessness, and the disproportionate incarceration of Black men for minor crimes.

I once gave a Ted Talk in which I spoke extensively about the experience of young Black people in the UK and the impact that society has on their growth. I described my upbringing in Zimbabwe and mentioned how everyone called me 'nherera' (orphan). I spoke about how strong the power of words can be and how sometimes those in authority or positions of control can forget this. I wished people would just call me by my name, allowing me to create my own identity. Even though I was young, I had some idea of what the term meant and began to feel sorry for myself. I would mimic how the adults responded when they heard my father had passed away and my mother was living in England. There was an element of sorrow when the term 'nherera' was used, so my young and impressionable self then adapted to that role. I drove home the fact that if we are to treat young people a certain way, they will most likely respond accordingly. Having young Black men constantly labelled in a negative manner and misrepresented in the media can have damaging and negative effects. When store clerks follow Black boys in the shop and treat them as suspects, it is hard to imagine how it must make them feel. Knowing that the history of stop and search in the UK centres mainly on Black boys raises cause for concern. These acts send out messages, messages that young people, especially young Black people, are not to be trusted, believed in or given a chance. By stereotyping and acting on prejudices, society is perpetuating dangerous narratives that are damaging to self-esteem, confidence and the overall trajectory of these young people's lives.

My favourite author, Chimamanda Ngozi Adichie, speaks excellently on the dangers of a single story and how damaging it can be both to those who hear it and those who are the subject of it. It can give people the wrong perception of a group of people or a place, and thus they will treat it or them accordingly. She gives an example of the single story of the continent of Africa. People speak of Africa as a country; they speak of it as one place with one people, one language and one culture. They forget that it is a complex and multicultural continent that is full of a deep history that differs from country to country. There are fifty-four countries in Africa, each of which is filled with various languages and dialects, ethnicities, religions and overall differing ways of life. The single story of Africa is damaging because it removes the voices of those who do not fit that narrative and it begins to fetishise those who do, removing the layers of depth away from the vast continent. It places people into a box and does not allow them to exist outside of it, as they are expected to behave according to their 'norm'. It reduces and limits people's rights to be their authentic selves if these narratives are perpetuated. This example can be applied to the way many young people are treated around the world. They are often stereotyped and not given the chance to write their own narrative or tell their own story. Young people like myself are put into a box and given little room to grow or to showcase their talents.

These are *all* issues that I care about equally and hope one day to pursue, but for *now* I'm focused on equality in education. So, do not panic and assume that you need to decide on one 'purpose' and make that your only focus for the rest of your life. It is, of course, equally fine if there is one thing you want to pursue forever. Truthfully, this is all about you and how you want to shape your life. As one of my all-time heroes Mrs Michelle Obama says, '*You are living life and are on a journey of **becoming**.*' Nothing has to be final. A great way to begin is by picking the thing you feel *most* passionate about and allowing that to be your focus for a little while. Then you can review and adjust as you go, depending on your interests.

I should probably add that I learned a thing or two about following your passion and purpose from the lady herself. It's a moment I really enjoyed and will cherish deeply in my heart for years to come. I had looked up to her for a long time but even more so when she launched her 'Let Girls Learn' initiative as First Lady of the United States of America. This was an initiative that I followed avidly and was extremely in awe of. Her dedication and commitment to helping give a voice to those around the world, who had been silenced for so long, inspired me. When she released her book, I immediately purchased it and fell even more in love with her story and her life thus far. I loved how the book centred on her journey to becoming and how she noted that she was still on that journey despite her outstanding accomplishments thus far. My deep admiration for her was known by those around me. When it was announced that she was coming to the UK as part of her book tour, my best friend, Malala, decided to surprise me with backstage passes at one of her appearances, since she was coming in the month of my birthday. I remember relaxing in her backstage guest room at the London venue and being filled with excitement. When Mrs Obama finally arrived, I remember how kind and attentive she was. She immediately came over to say hello to Malala and they briefly caught up about life. She then turned to me and gave me the biggest hug and asked how I was doing, how university was going and what my plans for the future with girls' education were. The conversation was incredible and I just remember love and warmth radiating from her. Something I took away from our conversation was how deeply encouraging she was. She heard me state my dreams about going to Harvard and working in policy reform for girls and she immediately told me I could do it. She was unwavering in her responses to what I was saying and left me feeling like I could be and do anything that I set my sights on. Her advice about doing the things we care about and extending a helping hand to those who need it stuck with me. Mrs Obama's ability to make me feel so seen and heard in the conversation was incredible and has created a positive lifelong memory that I will never forget. What I learned from that conversation was that with life you have to let your passion drive you. At the very same time, you don't have to box yourself into one area, you can care about multiple things at once. I also learned the power of unapologetically owning what you want to do. When I told her about my future goals around girls' education, her response was so powerful. She accepted it and as she spoke to me, her belief that I was going to achieve those goals was clear. Normally, people might question how or why it's really possible for others to do the things they say they want to do. Mrs Obama's ability to address me in the way that I had shown I wanted to be addressed filled me with confidence and excitement, and it's something I think is worth raising when others share their dreams with you: try to really hear them and give them the listening ear you'd hope they would give you.

Practical steps to identifying what's important now

As I have mentioned, I care about many things and have multiple interests, but if I want to act now, it's essential to hone in on what's important. So, after you've made a list of all the things that are important to you, or all the interests that you may have, write down your current focus, your end goal, any difficulties you might face and how you might overcome this.

1. **Current focus:** Currently, my focus is on education, international education policies and understanding how we work towards gender equality and equity.

2. **End goal:** To help reduce the number of girls out of school by ensuring that all children have access to a free, safe and *quality* education.

3. **Potential difficulties:** Lack of experience, not having the right contacts to gain access into this work, not having a strong enough voice alone to make any change.

4. **How to overcome them:**

   - Locate places that are fighting for girls' education by googling what is in your local area, or perhaps messaging someone you know who may have contacts in that line of work. You could even pop into your local charity shop and enquire with them about other charities they may know of that tackle your specific cause. This is a great way of exploring the various organisations out there because you don't know what you don't know, and talking to people can always bring new groups or opportunities to light that you may not have heard of.

   - Use social media platforms to connect and network with people in this field and ask for advice or coffee meetings. For example, there are Instagram pages, like mine @empoweredbyvee, or others that are similar such as @vybl, @worthofmouth, @supanetwork, @motivez, @theladderprojectldn and many others that will help you tap into a network of like-minded individuals. Joining these platforms can be extremely beneficial as they host numerous events on a monthly basis with successful people who could be in the profession you are seeking. These platforms spend their time finding opportunities for young adults that are often free of charge and accessible. Become a part of these networks by signing up to their mailing lists so that you can be the first to know about the various opportunities they promote, such as mentorship openings, internships, work experience, apprenticeships or even job vacancies. Attend their events, network with the people who you want to surround yourself with and see where it takes you. I promise you it will be helpful in understanding how to go about finding opportunities and a community.

- Finally, to tackle the issue of not having a strong enough voice, join others who are already doing this work and work as a team rather than as an individual. There is strength in numbers, and this gives you a chance to meet new and like-minded people. As mentioned above, by joining these free networks on Instagram and other social media platforms, you are introducing yourself to people who have similar interests and are on similar paths. This is good, it means that you can motivate each other; if you begin to struggle you can ask for help.

Now that you've got a sense of what your purpose is or what you want to pursue for now, you might begin to doubt yourself and start thinking, *what if I fail at it*? I've had people ask me this question a lot, '*But what if I fail Vee, what if I fail?*' Each time my response is the same, '*But what if you fly my friend, what if you fly?*' Trust me, I know it's easy to focus on potential failure because our brains are programmed to think the worst before the best. It is a natural thing to do, to scope out the risks before you make a move. But, in the case of following your dreams, you need to flip these thoughts on their head. Instead of only considering the worst-case scenario, equally consider the best. Seriously, think about it: what if your idea actually works? What if it hits a global market that you didn't even know existed and becomes the very thing the world has been waiting for? What if you end up becoming the leading expert in whatever your passion is? What if you go on to create something that changes people's lives on a generational scale? Just . . . what if?

The thing is, you'll never truly know unless you try. If you're coming from a place of pain and want to turn that into purpose, make sure you deal with those emotions first. Come to terms with the things that have happened and make sure you're on a journey of healing before you try to help others. More often than not we try to mask our pain by distracting ourselves, so to truly devote yourself to the work at hand, try to look after yourself first. Then, go ahead and gift the world with your passions and talents. Also, remember to reach out to others, build your community of support and start creating something magical. Being empowered is about living *your* life and doing it unapologetically; dreaming big in the pursuit of your passions and making lemonade out of lemons.

'BUT WHAT IF I FAIL VEE, WHAT IF I FAIL?'

EACH TIME MY RESPONSE IS THE SAME, 'BUT WHAT IF YOU FLY MY FRIEND, WHAT IF YOU FLY?'

Get it in Order

SETTING EMPOWERED LIFE GOALS

One of my all-time favourite tasks is sitting down in a cosy room with a fresh planner and writing down my goals for the beginning, middle, and end of the year. I love the art of goal setting, habit building, and system changing because it makes me feel extremely empowered and in control. I get to list the things I want to see come into fruition and then spend my days ensuring that it happens. I've been setting goals religiously for many years and they've become a dominant topic of discussion on my YouTube channel. The systems, views, and approaches that I take to setting my goals and how I view them has changed my life drastically. For so long I used to allow the years to pass me by, not knowing what I wanted until I literally started writing and speaking them into existence. I used to let life just happen to me as opposed to making it happen for myself. I was somewhat passive in my surroundings but one day decided this had to change.

THUS CAME THE BIRTH OF MY 'EMPOWERED LIFE GOALS'.

Why do I call them 'empowered life goals'? It's because I believe that every goal we set should contribute to bettering you, the people around you or the world that we live in. I believe that life is about the pursuit of peace, happiness, love, and your goals and desires. Your goal could be to be a Grammy-nominated musician, to help lead reform for girls' education, to become a wonderful parent to lots of children or to attend the best engineering school in the world. Whatever your goals are, they will inherently carry something you desire, something that will make you or those around you happy.

So, in some sense of the word, your goals, whether personal, collective, or global, should empower you or have elements of empowerment for others. Our goals can sometimes lack the empowerment element but be a means to an end, and the end is typically what we really want. For example, having to get a good grade in a class that you hate so you can attend the college you really want. The goals we set indicate what we want to pursue and pour our energies into for an extended period of time, so it's really important to know how to go about setting them and how to ensure you meet your desired objectives.

Something I always ask myself whenever I'm setting my goals is, why do I want this? What do I hope to see come from achieving this goal and how do I guarantee I stay on track?

Something I always ask myself whenever I'm setting my goals is, *why do I want this? What do I hope to see come from achieving this goal and how do I guarantee I stay on track?* There were moments in my life when I did things without purpose, with no understanding of why, and as you can imagine, I found it hard to find self-motivation or even enjoyment. One example is attending Art and Design classes in school. I had no desire to participate in these classes, my younger self did not see their purpose, and I simply didn't enjoy what I was learning. I often battled with myself to take an interest but my performance reflected this. These kinds of moments can become very frustrating very quickly. Despite my wish list incorporating the desire to pass these classes, I wasn't truly invested in them and didn't put a lot of effort into the goal. There were also other classes that I hated, such as Maths and Science, but I took a different approach to them because they carried a different value in my mind. I knew I needed to get good grades in these subjects to get into my desired sixth forms and colleges. This would then get me to my dream university and eventually my dream job. Therefore, my work ethic was drastically different because I could *see* the long-term outcome of achieving the good grades in them.

SO THE KEY HERE IS TO REMEMBER WHAT YOU WANT TO ACHIEVE, KEEP IT AT THE FOREFRONT OF YOUR MIND (WHILE ALSO ALLOWING ROOM FOR ALTERNATIVES IF YOUR CONTEXT, GOALS OR FINANCIAL SITUATION CHANGES) AND KEEP IN MIND YOUR PASSION FOR WHY YOU EVEN BEGAN THAT GOAL IN THE FIRST PLACE.

The pyramid system

This brings us to one of my favourite goal setting tools: the pyramid system. This is something I discuss endlessly on my YouTube channel and have used for a long time. This system allows me to see, at the start of the year, what my end goal is before breaking it down. The pyramid system essentially gives you an overview of what's at stake, so you know what you need to be doing throughout the year (or years) to get there.

- **The first step is taking your current goal and placing it at the top of the pyramid**; typically your pyramid will have about three rows. For example, my current big goal is reaching 250,000 subscribers on YouTube. This has been my goal for the past year, and one that has been on my mind a lot.

- **Next to your current goal, add an end date or month.** This date should be as realistic as possible because the last thing you want to do is set unrealistic and hopeful standards and then burn yourself out trying to meet them. So really sit and plan your dates for completing your goals as accurately as you can.

- **In the second row of the pyramid, break down where you need to be in the next six months**, split into two sections (three months each).

- **Below this, on the final row, write where you want to be in the other six months prior to the end goal**, broken down similarly into two sections (three months each).

One of the reasons why I love this pyramid system is because it continually breaks down your goals, from the end goal back to the current moment you're in.

This method can help you figure out what you need to be doing in the coming days, weeks and months for you to reach your end goal. This is helpful for me to make sure I'm on track to reach 250,000 subscribers. Every week I know I need to upload (at a minimum) one to two YouTube videos in order to gain a steady growth of subscribers. I need to be constantly thinking of new ways to engage with my current audience while attracting new ones. When I look at my pyramid goal, I know that today, I should be sitting down and planning, creating, or editing new videos to upload in order to meet my goal for that section of the pyramid.

There are many examples we could factor in here. Here, I've used the example of the process of buying a house.

- Let's imagine that to purchase the property, you need a deposit of £10,000 and that your aim is to save this in the coming two years. This means your goal for the first year will be to save at least £5,000. This is the figure you place at the top of your pyramid with the words 'buy a house' next to it.

- Below that, you might note that in the first six months of the year, you should have saved at least half of the required figure, or close to it. So, £2,500.

- Then below that, break down what each of those first six months should look like, where you should be setting a goal to put aside at least £400.00 a month.

- This should eventually bring you to the current day, where you should ask yourself, *what could I be doing to ensure I am getting to this goal? Should I consider finding alternative ways of travelling around with my friends? Instead of taking an Uber, maybe I should take the tube? Instead of ordering in as often as I do, why don't I sacrifice one of my takeaway days and meal prep in advance?* These small prompts that you factor in on a daily, weekly or monthly basis can be useful ways of meeting your monthly target.

The Quarter System

I used to say my goals were 'balanced' until I had a phone conversation with my friend George. He asked me if the term 'balanced' described the way I handled my tasks or handled my life in general, and upon reflection I realised it did not. I now, after some careful explanation from George, prefer to say my goals are in harmony. We are often taught, growing up, that we need to lead a balanced lifestyle, maintain a balanced diet, a balanced work/play routine and more, but this isn't entirely true. There will be times when we might need to eat more protein to build our muscles, or take more time off work because we have other projects happening, etc. The term 'balanced' implies that each goal and each part of our lives must be divided equally, but each goal in my life wasn't given an equal amount of time, attention, and care. Now I say that my goals are living in harmony with one another. They alternate between levels of importance depending on what takes priority during different moments of my life, something I've discussed at great length over the years.

Each section of my year is shaped by what goal takes the greatest priority during that time and what the desired outcome will be.

Each section of my year is shaped by what goal takes the greatest priority during that time and what the desired outcome will be. I break down each year based on the popular OKR (objectives and key results) model, better known to me as the Quarterly Goal System; the OKR goal system was created by Andy Grove in the 1970s but made popular by John Doerr, one of the earlier investors in Google. I've adapted this business-based model of goal achieving to fit my more personal and academic goals. The Quarterly Goal System helps me make my goals more specific to the season rather than just an overview of the year. It essentially gives me four 'New Year's Resolution' moments in one year. It helps me focus in on the details and breaks down the mammoth goals into bite-sized chunks, which are easier to handle.

- So, for example, instead of saying 'in 2022 I want to achieve X, Y, Z', you would put in Q1 of 2021 (Quarter 1 of 2021) 'I would like to achieve A, B and C in order to stay on track for the end of year goals X, Y and Z.

- The year is split into four quarters, Q1 representing January, February and March, Q2 April, May, and June and so on.

By using this system to break down the period, it means your goals don't have to be balanced. The time frames are broken down in a way that allows whatever needs priority to be the focus during different parts of the year. Another reason I have come to love the quarter system is because it allows for flexibility and readjustment in the way that the annual goal setting system does not. Essentially, it means each new quarter behaves like a 'new year'. Every three months you sit down and evaluate what went well, what did not and what needs to be improved moving forward into the next 'year', similar to the New Year's Resolutions you set for January 1, when you become a 'new you'. Combining the pyramid with the system of quarterly goals truly helps me with my bigger visions. I write my large goals into the top of my pyramids then every three months I review them, setting the smaller goals for that quarter and adjusting as I go. Sometimes, with each quarter I may find that the end goal needs to alter because my vision has changed based on how the previous quarter went, or there could be new things on the horizon that affect the climate of what I want to do.

THE TERM 'BALANCED' IMPLIES
THAT EACH GOAL AND EACH PART
OF OUR LIVES MUST BE DIVIDED
EQUALLY, BUT EACH GOAL IN MY
LIFE WASN'T GIVEN AN EQUAL
AMOUNT OF TIME, ATTENTION,
AND CARE. NOW I SAY THAT MY
GOALS ARE LIVING IN HARMONY
WITH ONE ANOTHER.

Dividing your goals into themes

Now, let me give you some real-life examples of how I typically set my goals. I like to begin by considering the different themes that matter to me. Each year they may alter slightly but generally I focus on five key areas: professional, academic, personal growth, social media, and health. These strands may look extremely similar and technically all intersect, but they are drastically different and require different things from me.

- My professional strand focuses on future career prospects, present work, and the things I'd like to do once I graduate and am no longer a student. This includes internships, work experience placements, volunteering, CV building, cover letters, interview prep, etc. All things that will prepare me for entering the working world.

- The academic strand, as you can imagine, centres around my education. This strand focuses on what my goals are for my grades, the things I'd like to learn, the schools I want to attend, assignments, exams and more. This is one of my biggest strands and takes the most focus. It's largely been dedicated to my time at Oxford and Harvard but also includes time studying courses outside of my university requirements, learning languages, doing voluntary research papers and more.

- The personal growth strand focuses around building my life skills, understanding things such as investing, taxes, saving money, learning how to drive, becoming more assertive and more confident, writing a book, etc. This strand centres on the things I personally want for myself that don't include anyone else.

- The social media strand is one that also takes up a lot of my time. This centres largely on my YouTube channel but is also broken down to include Instagram, LinkedIn, and Twitter. The goals in this strand usually focus on growth, but for me the most important thing is impact. It's a constant work in progress making sure all of the platforms are in harmony with an impactful and helpful message. I have to make sure they're constantly on brand but also a space where I can be my most authentic and creative self. Each quarter predicts what the channel should look like as it evolves and gains new audience members while maintaining the active ones. A lot of the goals in this strand focus on rebranding anything that may not be working, introducing new editing skills and different ways of becoming more efficient in producing meaningful and impactful content. This strand also focuses on the business aspect, the brand collaborations, finances, contracts, partnerships and more.

- Lastly, I have my health strand, which is arguably the most important. This one focuses on my mental, physical, and spiritual health. I also use this strand to include my family and personal relationships as I feel they contribute largely to my wellbeing. In this one I set targets for things such as how physically active I should be, my diet and my sleeping patterns. When you're in a world that requires you to be 'on' 24/7 it becomes easy to forget to take time off, sleep well, etc. When working on social media, you can easily stay online for hours on end and combined with a full-time Master's degree and a YouTube channel, things can become overwhelming very quickly. I love this strand the most because it forces me to stop and reflect on how I truly feel. You can't do your best if you don't feel your best. For me to show up and create great content or perform well in an academic assignment, I need to make sure my mental health is taken care of. I strongly believe that all our goals rest on our health. The kinder we are to the bodies and minds we want to use to achieve these incredible goals, the better the journey becomes. Because of this, a large factor of each quarter is understanding where I am mentally and focusing everything around that.

A recent example is the process of producing this book. I decided that Q1 of the year would focus solely on the book and a social media detox. Hence, I came offline from all of my platforms, a complete blackout for two to three months. This was something that I've *never* done before. The reason I made this decision was because I knew that mentally I couldn't handle a full-time Harvard degree, writing a book, and also maintaining a full-time social media presence. Something had to give.

The first step to making your dreams a reality

Let's talk about how to actually be prepared for what you are about to speak into existence. I am a firm believer in the classic mantra that success is when opportunity meets preparation. I have always 'dressed how I want to be addressed' and as I mention in my introduction, I use that term very lightly to mean approach life as you want it to approach you. In essence, when I set my goals, I start behaving as if they are mine, my mindset alters, and I start pouring my energy into manifesting them into existence. If you are a person of faith this might centre on praying about it or putting it as the focus of your fasting in the new year. If you aren't a person of faith, you might write in your diary, wish for guidance from the universe, or maybe even speak to your friends and family about it. Whichever approach you take, make it real for yourself and start speaking it into existence, then acting on it.

I remember for so long I wanted to work with LinkedIn. They had been one of my dream brands for a long time. I had no idea how I'd end up working with them and in what capacity, but I had them loud and proud on my vision board. I decided to incorporate them into the things I was already doing, so that when the time came, I was ready. I verbally expressed how much I enjoyed the app on my social media platforms. Whenever I hosted my annual access event, I taught a LinkedIn session and showed students how to maximise their skills, potential, and opportunities through the platform. The talks were always the students' favourite section because of how similar the platform is to Facebook. We taught students how to network, how to pitch themselves or their businesses, and how to use social media to their professional advantage. The genuine enthusiasm for the platform showed through the students' use of it after our sessions and also reflected in the way that I posted about how helpful I had found LinkedIn to gain information about the world of work.

So, when a few years later my manager told me they had reached out to work with me on a year-long campaign, I was ecstatic. All my unsolicited work with LinkedIn and the constant tagging of the platform on my social media networks had prepared me for this opportunity. It made me confident in my knowledge of the brand and in how I would want to work with them. When I sat down with two team members who were working on the campaign, I made sure they knew about every last detail of what I had been doing with the brand prior to any collaboration, and shared how much I loved the platform. They explained that the campaign was about making change in the world of work for underrepresented students. I had been selected as one of their seven Changemakers in the UK and we became the faces of the campaign featuring in video ads globally across Instagram, YouTube, LinkedIn and Twitter. My decision to put working with LinkedIn into my vision board had prepared me for this opportunity. My continued references to LinkedIn and organically sharing how much I loved their network had given me an advantage in that I was able to raise my profile with them and get noticed as a good choice to work with. It made my collaboration with the brand a lot easier because I was genuinely enthusiastic and had manifested the moment.

I AM A FIRM BELIEVER IN THE CLASSIC MANTRA THAT SUCCESS IS WHEN OPPORTUNITY MEETS PREPARATION.

Practical steps to get it in order

1. Write it down. Write down your goals, desires, and the changes you would like to make. To achieve it is to see it. It's really important that you can see these goals, not just keep them in your mind. I also believe that there's something in writing it to believe it. When you write it down you begin to believe it can happen because a part of it now exists in the universe outside of your mind. Verbally manifesting your ideas also helps. When you speak it you feel it. I recall so many moments when I said an idea out loud and something about the words circling my space gave me the energy I needed to pursue that goal because now it felt tangible.

   - Writing your goals down also helps with being able to tick them off, or delete them when you'd like to adjust or re-evaluate them. It also helps keep you accountable. If you haven't written it down or added it to your calendar, it doesn't exist.

   - Once you have your goals in writing, make sure you make a habit of actually looking at them on a regular basis. Read back your own words and your own vision. You owe it to yourself to actually put your words into action and get started. Writing them down and closing your notebook for five months is not going to help. You have to actively engage with your thoughts, look over them, check where you should be in the timeline and adjust as you go. For me, I wake up every morning, go to my desk, open my planner and look at my daily to-do list, otherwise I genuinely don't know what I need to do for the day. On a weekly basis I check in with my quarterly goals and every two weeks or so, I double check my longer-term plans.

2. **Create systems to make your life easier.** The next thing
I would recommend is creating systems first and tying
them into your goals. It's worthless to simply put 'study
more and get good grades' and just wake up every single
day to go and spend hours sitting in a library not actually
knowing what you are doing.

- Put in place a system that addresses your learning
  style and preferred study method. If that is ensuring
  you are going to sleep on time, waking up at a decent
  time, exercising regularly, or sitting in a cafe to study
  because the library makes you sleepy, then so be
  it. Understand what the issue is first, then create a
  system that helps you get there. Putting things in
  place that can help you save time and avoid bad habits
  makes more sense. Essentially, using systems to line
  up your goals is like taking the prevention vs cure
  approach in life. Before the issue even occurs, there
  will be systems in place to avoid it.

- An example of this could be your health. You may only
  want to write down 'maintain a healthy weight' on your
  goal list but this wouldn't be helpful because it doesn't
  speak to a process, a system or a new habit. You
  want to create new habits in order to turn them into a
  lifestyle. For example, you could say something like,
  'walk 10,000 steps a day,' 'eat five fruits a day,' 'don't
  buy high sugar foods or have them in the house.' These
  make your end goals more realistic because you're
  building systems and habits around them. Instead of
  saying 'don't eat unhealthy food constantly', it might
  be better to understand what makes you feel tempted
  to do so, and address that, or try a more balanced
  weekly shop to slowly adjust to eating a better diet.

Also, try learning to cook healthier food in bulk, especially with friends and family to make the process more fun, and explore healthier options that are similar to what you normally enjoy. Find new systems that can help to tackle the goal you have in mind in such a way that it eventually becomes a lifestyle.

- Sit down with the goals you initially wrote, and write down the practical systems you can put in place to make sure everything you're doing works towards building habits that will become a lifestyle. Whether the goals are work related, health focused, or just for personal growth, you must build systems around them to uphold them, especially when things get difficult and you get tempted to give up.

3. Make your goals manageable. Lastly, break down your goals, desires, and systems into bite-size chunks. The more easily manageable each step of this is, the easier it becomes to achieve. The last thing you want to do is frighten yourself out of pursuing your dream.

- Writing down 'write a 50,000 word book by the end of the year' isn't helpful. It will scare you and the closer the time gets the more worried you will become and the more likely you are to want to remove that goal out of fear.

- As mentioned in the Quarterly Goal System section, it's good if you can cut your yearly goals into four chunks or four quarters: Q1, Q2, Q3 and Q4. Doing this allows you to see that 50,000-word writing goal as 12,500 words per quarter which, when broken down into months, is about 4,000 words per month.

- Breaking it down makes the goal much more manageable and closer to reality. It allows you to see the bigger picture up close and personal. So now you know that you will need to write about 250 words every few days to make sure that by the end of the year you have 50,000 words for your book. It means you can shape your daily life around your goal in a less intimidating way.

Overall, just remember that everything you desire is within your reach. Sometimes not in the exact time frame that you want; it may take an extra year or five, but it's the getting there that counts. The journey of reaching your goals or dreams is just as important as the goals or dreams themselves. Remember to take your time, and to be kind to yourself. It's okay to alter your goals as you go along because you're a multifaceted human being who grows and evolves constantly.

IT'S ALSO OKAY TO FEEL DISAPPOINTED IF YOU DON'T REACH THE DESIRED GOAL TO BEGIN WITH. TRY AGAIN! START A NEW SYSTEM TO GET THERE, EVALUATE YOUR STRENGTHS, WEAKNESSES, WHAT WENT WELL AND WHAT DID NOT.

You deserve to enjoy the things you desire and the best things that life has to offer. Just keep going, keep setting those goals, applying those systems, and building new habits, and watch the magic unfold!

Rejection is Redirection

STAYING EMPOWERED AFTER REJECTION

I OFTEN SAY, REJECTION IS REDIRECTION AND FAILURE IS JUST ANOTHER CHANCE TO TRY AGAIN. I SAY THIS BECAUSE I TRULY BELIEVE IT.

The more I've repeated the phrase to myself over the years, the easier life has become. Moments that I would've otherwise perceived as moments of downfall now live in my mind as moments of greatness. What I mean is that whatever happens in life *happens*, but what matters most in that moment is how we deal with it and, most importantly, how we mark it in our minds. My good friend George puts it perfectly, it's all about 'how you frame it', and I couldn't agree more. You may get rejected from the job you applied for. The business idea you have might not quite go to plan during the pitching stages. You can look at these two events as moments of failure because you tried and technically did not 'succeed'. You may have even had everything riding on those moments, and not receiving the funding for your business idea, or getting the position you applied for may discourage you and leave you feeling deflated.

The actual feeling of rejection may inspire fear and you may want to give up and never speak of your idea again. I understand why you would feel this way. This is human nature; we internalise things because we often seek validation from the things that we do or strive for. When receiving a rejection, you may take it as an ultimate rejection of *you*. If we take George's advice, however, and reframe the moment, you could look at it as a learning curve. This can be your chance to take your idea back to the drawing board and innovate it. Some employers are kind enough to give feedback about why you did not get the role, but if they don't, make sure you chase it up.

Find out what did not work for them and ensure that issue is addressed before you apply for your next job. What you might find is that there's a little thing that needs tweaking. If other employers have noticed this, it could be impacting their hiring decision.

I've been in this situation myself. I applied for many scholarships for my Master's degree at Harvard and received rejections from every single one of them. Even the ones that weren't as competitive said 'no' to me. Every single one. Of course, I did not get feedback from the majority of them but the one that did, which was the one I really wanted, was extremely insightful. They let me know the reason: despite my passion for my subject and my bright future prospects, I was lacking experience. They felt that there were more qualified students who had years' worth of experience that were applying for Master's degrees in subjects that were aligned with their current roles. I, however, was still figuring things out and finding my way. They told me I should reapply the following year, after taking time to undertake work experience outside of my studies (I was going straight from undergrad to postgrad). I still went ahead with my overall application and got into my university of choice but I obviously didn't have a scholarship. Not having a scholarship made things extremely difficult. I now had to raise all of the funds needed for my education on my own. I knew it would be hard but I was determined to make it work. My point here is, without the feedback I received, I would have continued to think my rejection was due to not being good enough.

> *Something I always ask myself whenever I'm setting my goals is, why do I want this? What do I hope to see come from achieving this goal and how do I guarantee I stay on track?*

Their response showed me that it was something as simple as experience. They were not saying *no*, they were saying *not right now* and provided a valid reason *why*. And, in their defence, I can understand why these scholarships rejected me; I did not appear as prepared, organised or practised as the others. I was going up against applicants who were much older and more experienced than me – from heads of international schools across the globe to those who had worked for the United Nations or served as government officials in their respective countries. The scholarships I was applying for were prestigious, and would essentially be giving away close to $80,000 per student. This is a lot of money and a huge investment to put into someone. Naturally, the bright-eyed graduate whose experience only stretches as far as YouTube and her student campus may not stand as tall next to a former UNICEF exec.

Once I had received the feedback, it sat well with me. I mean, I didn't agree that to study what you care about, you should need to have extensive experience, but I understood where they were coming from and could rationalise the advice. And, if I were to take a year out, which I did not, I would've ensured my next round of applications focused more on experience than future aspirations. I would have spent that year volunteering at my local educational institutions and guaranteeing that I had more to discuss in my interviews.

So, whenever you can, ask for feedback, either from the employers themselves or even from your most honest friends and family. Present to them what you presented to the organisations you were applying for, ask them to read your CV/cover letter, and even consider getting them to interview you – all of this can help. These moments will provide you with useful insight, particularly into how you come across to others. We might think we're communicating one thing, but those listening can hear something else entirely. For example, with

WHENEVER YOU CAN, ASK FOR FEEDBACK, EITHER FROM THE EMPLOYERS THEMSELVES OR EVEN FROM YOUR MOST HONEST FRIENDS AND FAMILY.

those Harvard scholarship applications, I had decided
to speak so much about what I *wanted* to do in the future and
the change I wanted to see in the world, that I actually ended
up downplaying the things I *had* accomplished while taking
a full-time degree. At the time, I thought my future goals
mattered more. However, those offering the scholarships
wanted 'proof', if you may, of how committed I already was
to my cause and how I had already contributed to that field.
I assume that the interviews, personal statements and
applications I sent off read as if I was someone who woke
up one day and randomly decided to apply for a prestigious
scholarship with no prior experience in the field. When it came
to writing the university application statement (you send the
scholarship forms a month before the actual application),
I had sent a draft to my principal – the phenomenal Alan
Rusbridger – and he told me the same thing. He said, 'Vee,
I've seen the incredible work you have done here at Oxford
and with prospective students. Where is more of that in your
application?' When I received the sponsorship feedback a few
weeks later, I realised I wasn't presenting myself in the way
I thought I was. We made sure my actual Harvard personal
statement spoke more to what I had done and my experience.
I cannot say for sure that I got into Harvard because of
the changes I made to my statement. All I know is that the
feedback has stuck with me and now I ask myself what am I
trying to say and how is it *actually* coming across.

TAKING ON FEEDBACK EITHER FULLY OR WITH A PINCH OF SALT HELPS YOU START TO SEE REJECTION AS REDIRECTION TO SOMETHING GREATER, SOMETHING YOU DIDN'T EVEN KNOW YOU NEEDED. HAVING THE SKILL OF REFRAMING AND SEEING OPPORTUNITY FOR IMPROVEMENT – EVEN IN THE MOMENTS THAT DISAPPOINT YOU – CAN HELP YOU GET A STEP CLOSER TO LIVING YOUR DREAMS.

Let's say that your application for funding was declined. You request feedback, and you're told that the model you presented didn't identify a gap in the market. You now have the chance to go away and adjust your idea to include the new and competitive elements it was missing and the next time you pitch it, the investors are likely to be blown away. The job rejection you received might now give you insight into what companies are looking for, based on what the employers said you might have lacked in the interview process. You now get to go and work on those skills so that next time you apply, you are an even stronger candidate. As a result, you will have now brushed up on, or gained, skills you may have overlooked previously. You may also realise that the role you were applying for may have ended up being incompatible with your interests, thus saving you years in a job you may not enjoy. That moment of rejection then redirects you to greater things. Even though it sounds cliché (a common theme in this book!) when 'one door closes, another one literally opens'. It's also worth bearing in mind that these things don't happen overnight. Some people become lucky by being in the right place at the right time or just happen to know the right person to make their dreams come true. But this isn't the reality for the majority of people, and to get something we have to work for it. I'm not saying work hard and boom, your dreams come true! I'm saying that it's going to take time. It may take a few years before the world believes in your idea. It may take fifty rejections before the right door for you will open. The journey will be exhausting and you will be tested along the way, but I promise

I'm not saying work hard and boom, your dreams come true! I'm saying that it's going to take time. It may take a few years before the world believes in your idea. It may take fifty rejections before the right door for you will open.

it will be so worth it in the end. Now let me share my moment of 'rejection' that ended up redirecting me and changing my life as I knew it.

When barriers are put in your way

My biggest moment of rejection came whilst I was in the world of academia. I had spent my final year of A-Levels working extremely hard to try to get the best grades possible so that I could attend the university of my dreams. My mum instilled in me the idea that education is a ticket to a good life. She always told me it was one thing that people could not take away from me. So, when the time came, I began searching on the internet for various universities available to me and the different courses I might want to study. At the time I had three As from my first-year exams, so figured I could apply to any UK university since I met the highest entry requirements. I had my heart set on two places, Exeter and Oxford, with a preference for Exeter. They both had wonderful history degree programmes and included a year abroad, something that made travel-hungry teen Vee want to die with excitement. After visiting a few of my university selections, I had my five choices set. I approached my teacher to ask for help with the process, get references and things of this nature. Before I go ahead with my story, I want to make a disclaimer: our sixth form was great and my friends and I had a great time there. Many of the staff truly did do their best to support their students with the resources that they had available. I made lifelong friends, learned new skills, and grew a new layer of resilience; however, sometimes my peers and I felt overlooked and unaccommodated, and we often had in-depth conversations about how we felt. When the time came to apply for university, a lot of us felt nervous about the extent of the support that we would receive. I think it's safe to say that we didn't feel as pushed as we would've liked.

I remember nervously asking one of my teachers what they thought about me applying to Oxford and if they could help. I will never forget their initial reaction, which was, of course, later corrected. Maybe they were having a bad day or something else was on their mind, but in essence they told me no. The teacher kindly let me know, in words that I will remember as clear as day for the rest of my life, that Oxford wasn't for people like 'us'. By that I think they meant the area we were in and my socioeconomic background. I never asked for clarification. I didn't need to. I remember feeling so heartbroken and annoyed by their dismissal and lack of approval. I was even more annoyed that their approval mattered to me so much. I felt annoyed because everything in my life up until that point had been a battle and when I heard that particular 'no', I felt exhausted by the prospect of entering another battle to prove myself, another battle to show that I was worthy of what I desired.

My educational journey oftentimes required me to fight for my teachers' attention. Teachers questioned my intelligence, made excuses for why I had performed well or told me to slow down for reading too quickly and getting ahead of others. It felt like they hated the fact that I picked things up quickly, almost as if it was going against what they had expected for me. I was constantly dealing with adversity, whether being mocked for my accent and pronunciation while learning English, fighting to be put in the correct classes, or having to beg teachers to call out the blatant racism I was experiencing in classes that somehow always went unpunished. In that moment, when my teacher dismissed my wish to apply to Oxford – without even considering why I wanted to do it or the fact that I met their requirements – I felt tired. That moment represented all the moments I had felt let down by the education system.

It's extremely important to understand that for a student like myself who migrated to the UK, had to learn English, came from a single-parent household, is Black and working class, the *last* thing I needed to hear that day was 'no'. The 'no' was another way for society to tell me that I had failed the race of life before I had even begun. It reinforced the fears I had of sharing my idea with her to begin with. It reinforced the feelings of being overlooked that my friends and I spoke about endlessly in Chicken Hut during our lunchtimes. It meant to me that the stereotypes I had embedded in my mind about what success and a bright future looked like were sadly true. For a student like myself, who did not, at that time, know someone who had attended Oxbridge, this did not feel like the end of the journey. I could not turn on the TV and see another young Black girl discussing her journey applying for top universities. If anything, what I saw about people like myself on TV was typically negative and unfair. What I needed to hear at that time was words of encouragement, to be told that the sky (and beyond) was the limit. My teacher's opinion mattered. I could not go home and ask my mum for help as she did not understand UCAS or the UK system of applying to university. That 'no', in my developing world, truly meant no. What makes me sad to this day is that I had the grades. I had the passion. What I didn't have was the support.

Nonetheless, I tried my best to go forward with my application and finally found some help from our careers advisor (a truly incredible woman who did her best to help me and genuinely believed in me) but I still felt demoralised by my teacher and sadly did not apply that year. The thought that I had let my dream fade ate away at me for a long time. For the rest of the academic year, my friends would ask me why I had not just done it. Why I had not just found a way and believed in myself more. They reminded me that it was important for students like us to prove these teachers wrong and show the world what we were made of.

But, although it wasn't a direct rejection from the institution Oxford itself, the 'no' from my teacher and her lack of faith in my abilities had done the job. The following year, a lot of things went wrong at our sixth form, including teachers falling ill, dealing with family issues, or leaving due to more promising job offers. We were given an endless string of replacement teachers, some lasting only two weeks while others specialised in different subjects to the ones they were teaching us. My friend Lauren and I still reminisce about how one of our teachers would tell us about their dream job while they were in class teaching us. Lauren and I would make bets before the class about how many times we thought the teacher would mention their dream role; it genuinely became a game for us. Staying motivated in that environment became difficult as it was clear that our on-again, off-again teachers were mainly concerned with just getting us to pass rather than pushing us to our full potential. I also remember being placed in a class in which I had achieved an A grade for the previous year. I was sitting next to a boy who had achieved a D grade, and our teacher was therefore teaching us at C grade standard to ensure those on the lower-grade pipeline were given a chance to secure a B (or a pass grade). This decision meant, no matter what I did in that class, my vision for an A* was not going to happen. I was not being taught at A* level. My friends and I felt as if we were doomed and ended up hosting our own after school clubs, teaching ourselves the materials and praying that we made it out of sixth form with good grades.

Things took a massive turn for the better when I was preparing for my end of year exams. This was when my unexpected moment of redirection came to me. I received an email from the Social Mobility Foundation telling me about a pioneering course that was happening at Lady Margaret Hall, Oxford University, called the Foundation Year. The programme was aimed at students who wanted to attend a place like Oxford but felt that, because of external barriers, they could not. Every aspect of the email spoke to me and my situation and I immediately felt compelled to apply. The first thought that came to my mind was that I was extremely worried about 'wasting time', something that a different teacher at my college had warned me about when I explained my desire to now apply for the Oxford Foundation Year. She thought I was a bright girl who was wasting her time doing this course when I could be starting my undergrad studies at Exeter immediately after my sixth form studies. You see, the small loophole with the Foundation Year was that it had no guarantee of progression onto the 'actual' Bachelor's degree at Oxford. It was a year created to help prepare you for undergrad studies at any top UK university and give you the support you had missed out on during your sixth form years. Many people around me worried about what would happen if, after one year, I didn't get in. Looking back now, I'm deeply saddened that this was ever an idea presented to me. It saddens me that not taking the conventional route was considered a 'waste of time'. It's a narrative preached to so many young people via social media or by figures of authority, as if there's only one way to live life, and anything outside of this is considered a 'waste'.

After hearing everyone's thoughts and deeply regretting not applying for Oxford the first time around, I decided to follow my heart and grab the opportunity that the universe was bringing to me. I spoke to my mum, my number one supporter, and she told me that no matter what the outcome of my year at Oxford was, it could never be a 'waste of time'. She told me to stop being afraid of the unknown and to learn to be flexible and grab opportunities when they present themselves. She told me to ignore those at church and at college who said I would be 'a year behind my peers' or that I was taking too much of a gamble by applying to something so new and pioneering. The thing is, I deeply believe that anything you do that helps you to advance your skills, increase your knowledge, discover your passions, or explore different options is NOT a waste of time. If anything, these are some of the most valuable moments of your life. It's really important to take risks, try things out and figure out what you want. This was how my mother and I saw it, and based on this logic, when that email fell into my inbox, I had to overcome my fears and apply, despite what those around me would think about the decision. Acceptance into the programme meant I would become one out of ten of the first students to undergo the very first Foundation Year at Oxford or Cambridge. I was about to go on to make history at one of the oldest universities in the world as the first Black student to be accepted into Oxford through a foundation year and I didn't even know it.

> *The thing is, I deeply believe that anything you do that helps you to advance your skills, increase your knowledge, discover your passions, or explore different options is NOT a waste of time. If anything, these are some of the most valuable moments of your life.*

When the acceptance letter arrived, I was thrown off guard because I really didn't expect it. I was also living in a different time zone, deep in the woods of Pennsylvania (I was doing Camp America at the time). The phone connection was poor and I remember desperately trying to get through to my mother, who was in England. When she finally picked up, I cried. To this day, I'm not sure why I was so overcome with emotion. I think I suddenly remembered the journey I had walked – from losing my father, my mother moving away, living with different family members who didn't want me, facing racism at school, my teacher telling me I wasn't good enough for a place like this and so much more. It felt, in that moment, like the universe had somehow reset the balance and the good was beginning to outweigh the bad.

I CALL THIS MY MOMENT OF REDIRECTION BECAUSE THE VERY DECISION TO APPLY FOR THIS PROGRAMME LITERALLY CHANGED THE COURSE OF MY LIFE FOREVER.

The Foundation Year genuinely restored my faith in my academic abilities and my passion for learning. They stripped everything back to the basics, so rather than writing an essay straight away, we were given access to a study skills guru, Dr Margaret Coombe, who helped us learn how to actually write an essay to begin with. She taught us how to read an academic book, how to break down essay questions and things of this nature. I know these things sound simple and intuitive but you'd be surprised at what bad habits you can pick up throughout your academic journey, so starting from scratch can be extremely helpful. I still use the skills I learned during my Foundation Year in 2016 to complete my work for my Master's programme.

Full disclosure about my A-level results: I had, unsurprisingly, received B grades for my final year, something I saw coming due to the lack of stability at our college that year. I was truly surprised I had not failed. At first, people at my church mocked me for not achieving A*s as they believed that As and A*s were the only acceptable grade for a smart student. But I chose to see my B grades as something beautiful. They were earned in a difficult environment, one that was not built to accommodate me fully, one that wanted to see me pass instead of excel. As I often say, I had been counted out of the race before I had even started. My Bs were earned through blood, sweat and tears, while working at McDonalds, volunteering part time and dealing with a line-up of teachers that didn't understand me or want to teach me. My Bs are golden and phenomenal and I continue to hold them with pride, honour, and utmost respect. I think knowing that the teaching side of things had not gone well may be the reason why I was so worried about my place on the Foundation Year, hence the tears of relief when I was accepted. The fear also came from knowing that if I lost my place at Oxford, I would lose my place at the other institutions since they were asking for higher requirements than the Foundation Year. My personal statement, grades and passion earned me a place on the Foundation Year.

My journey at Oxford University began on September 25th, 2016, and I took a chance at making my future brighter. I had no idea that grabbing the Foundation Year opportunity would become the catalyst for so many of the incredible things that have happened to me now. As you know from the first chapter, attending Oxford gave birth to my YouTube channel and a thriving social media presence. I don't think these things would've happened if I hadn't followed my intuition. My time at university encouraged me to fight for diversity and inclusion because I faced a lack of it in very glaring ways. I met other students who were like-minded and our passion for equal opportunities drove us to advocating for access into education. And, who knows, I may not be sitting here writing this very book that you are reading now. Although my rejection didn't come in the form of a 'we regret to inform you' letter from Oxford, it still impacted me in a similar way. The 'no' from my teacher ironically became the fuel that I needed to go on and prove her wrong and prove myself right. I knew I was capable and I knew I was smart; I just needed the support and encouragement. And, despite my hesitation and imposter syndrome when I first received the email about the Foundation Year, I knew deep down that this would be a life-changing opportunity that I needed to take.

So, what I'm saying to you is, whatever form of rejection you may receive on your journey, try and use it as fuel for your next move. Flip it on its head, find the positive and use it as a jug for the lemonade you are about to make. See it as a moment to grow, to try something else, and to come back stronger and more determined than ever. Taking the things you once thought were forms of 'rejection' or 'failure' and framing them in a positive light is ridiculously important. Knowing that you have the power to do this is also an important part of the self-empowerment journey. Learn how to take control of moments that may initially have been out of your control. Consider what those moments taught you, how they prepared you for the next chapter of your life, and how they have contributed to building your resilience, your character, and your strength.

> *So, what I'm saying to you is, whatever form of rejection you may receive on your journey, try and use it as fuel for your next move.*

Failure is another chance to try again

The second part of my mantra 'rejection is redirection' is that any form of 'failure is another chance to try again'. The notion of trying again is slightly different to redirection – the latter requires patience and waiting for the moment when you're guided to something greater. The notion of trying again requires you to take direct action. When something you've created has been rejected, go away, work on it some more, and try again (think of the earlier examples of the job interview or business plan not going to plan).

Another important point to note is that these ideas, plans, and business models are not *you*. These are things that you are creating but they are not you. When things go slightly 'wrong' and you need to readjust, this doesn't mean that you're inadequate. It simply means that the model needs re-evaluating. I typically place the term 'failure' in quotation marks because the older I've gotten, the more I believe that there's no such thing as actual 'failure'. I realise that this is a rather idealistic approach; however, I stand by it. I think that every moment we experience perceived 'failure' is the universe's way of telling us to rethink our model, idea, or plans.

Essentially any time that an idea faces 'failure' it's because either you, the idea, or the timing may just not be correct. This isn't a form of failure in my eyes, rather a moment just to re-evaluate, readjust, and try again. This part of the mantra requires resilience and perseverance. Whenever your first plan doesn't work, it's important to bounce back and try again but try again better. Bring new ideas to the table, take some risks, and give it your best shot. It's so easy to give up when things don't work out; trust me, I've been there. But it's important to remember that by giving up, you're ending the story. The book is over at chapter one. You must always be ready and willing to give yourself a whole and complete book of life. You deserve happiness, and happiness often takes effort, patience and time. So, refusing to try again when something 'fails' is to deprive yourself of the opportunity to experience the things you love and care about. You must ask yourself: don't you *want* and *deserve* to see what could (and will) happen in chapter two of your story if you keep on going? Yes, you may have to start afresh, but you will never know what could be if you never truly try. I mean really try, like sticking at it for a while despite the knockbacks. It's important to see yourself as the driver of the boat of *your* life. You decide which way to steer, and if there are harsh winds, find a new route and stay on track to your destination.

Practical steps to framing rejection as redirection and seeing failure as another chance to try again

1. Separate yourself from the product or the goal. When you detach your self-worth from the goal, you will make the process of accepting the moment of rejection much easier. By doing this, you're already setting yourself up for the redirection. It also helps you see it as something to learn from and to use as a source of strength.

2. Break down your ideas, plans, and business pitches into smaller steps and sections. This will help ensure that you are moulding as you go along, so if something doesn't work or you face rejection, it's far easier to retrace your steps and adjust as you go – it can be disheartening throwing out an entire idea.

3. Speak to yourself the way you would to someone you love and care about. Whenever something doesn't go

according to plan, before you begin to tell yourself you're not worthy enough or that you've failed as a person, ask yourself this: would you say the same thing to your younger cousin? Would you genuinely see them not getting an offer at their dream university as a reflection of them and their character? Would you tell your friend to give up and stop trying after not getting the job offer they wanted? I hope the answer to these questions is 'no'. If so, then why should you ever think of yourself in such a way? The answer to that one is, you shouldn't. Like I said earlier, it's absolutely crucial that you detach yourself personally from the outcome of the goal. The goal cannot be what you base your self-worth on. Therefore, whenever a moment of perceived 'failure' or 'rejection' occurs, treat yourself the same way you would someone you care for. The important thing is not allowing that emotion at being rejected to *become* you or to control you. Feel it, reframe it, dust yourself off and then try again.

4. Have accountability partners, people who you trust and who are honest with you and have your best interests at heart. I have a few friends that I trust with my ideas and believe will always give me honest and constructive feedback because they care about me. I trust my friends and family members no matter what, and I know that they want to see me happy, but they also want to see me do well. When I present my ideas to them, they will tell me the constructive truth. Having this form of support will help you get used to hearing the flaws in your plans and ideas and build up your resilience. This will help you if you need to take some time away to readjust your ideas. This way, you will be willing to try again, and NOT see it as a reflection of you.

Your accountability partners should also help you remain focused on your goal and not allow you to give up. They should become your second, third, and fourth pairs of eyes and ears for your projects, and help you brainstorm and innovate. Whenever I go to my friends with an idea, they always see the bigger picture and help me stop downplaying my ideas. They push me and create safe spaces for me, in which I can bounce my ideas off them without feeling judged or crazy. We will cover more about accountability partners in the 'Lean on Them' chapter (see page 92). If you have people like this in your life, open up to them, let them support you and I promise it will help you on your journey.

5. Seek other opportunities. In the same breath as having accountability partners, if you really feel what you were pursuing is no longer for you, do not be afraid to reach out to your network and seek new opportunities. As stated by Mrs Michelle Obama, the journey of becoming does have a definitive end. It's about *you* discovering *yourself*, the things you like and do not like. If that rejection is confirmation for you to leave the idea alone, that is also okay – just as long as it's not based simply on the fact that it was rejected. Perhaps the rejection highlighted you are not as passionate about the product or that there is something else you want to pursue. This is all okay, just as long as you take control of your life and do what feels right.

6. Trust the process. You might spend months applying for jobs and get rejected from fifty before you land your dream one (hopefully with a dream salary too!). Imagine if you had given up at rejection number forty-eight, or took a random offer because you were tired of trying? You'd have missed out on what was right for

you! Essentially, don't just 'trust the process', trust *your* process. I know it's much easier said than done, as is much of the advice I give, but trust me, it's true. Your process will not be the same as someone else's, it is *your* journey. Just because that particular route worked out for Lucy down the road does not mean it will for you as well, and vice versa. Yes, there are things you could do in the meantime – whether it's doing up your CV again or brushing up on your hard and soft skills – but overall, you must trust *your* process and *your* timing.

Overall, just please remember that you are human. It's inevitable that we make some mistakes in our work, that our plans may have some flaws. This is normal. It's common for your ideas to be changed and re-modelled ten times or more before they launch or are accepted. You are most likely reading the 707th draft of this book. Just kidding, it's not that many but it sure does feel like it! It's normal to face rejection a few times before things pick up. What matters is that you try again and try harder. To reach your end goal is incredible, but to embrace the process and the journey is even better. This is where the learning will really happen and where your strength will be built. So, repeat after me: rejection is redirection and failure is another chance to try again.

Am I Good Enough?

Enough?

HOW TO FEEL EMPOWERED IN THE FACE
OF IMPOSTER SYNDROME

The people who approach me feeling immense imposter syndrome are often people who come from backgrounds like mine. They are young Black or ethnic minority students, some of them raised in a single-parent household, from a lower socioeconomic background, who went to a poorly funded school, and were on free school meals. Sometimes they are girls in male-dominated environments, or students who have learned English as their second language or have attended university on a scholarship. Typically, these people feel most insecure about claiming their space in their new highly paid job role or top university.

Before I continue, I need to define what imposter syndrome is, to make sure we're on the same page and that we attach the correct word to the correct feeling. Imposter syndrome is essentially the overwhelming and constant feeling of 'I am not good enough', 'I do not belong', or 'they have made a mistake'. It's the constant self-doubt of occupying a space that you have rightfully earned. Imposter syndrome often kicks in when someone gains something that they either thought they would never gain or have been told by others they should be shocked they have gained. My getting into both Oxford and Harvard came as a big shock to myself, but also to those around me. Whenever I tell people where I study or have studied, their response tells me that my occupation of a space at that institution is something I should be amazed by. You would not experience imposter syndrome, for example, over being a good sibling. You would know whether you were kind, and would happily receive your sibling's praise without doubting yourself. You may, however, doubt yourself when given a promotion or a multimillion-dollar fund to oversee. I'll stop now because I think you get the gist, but essentially imposter syndrome is the doubting of your own skills and achievements because you fear that you may be exposed for being underqualified, despite earning your place.

IMPOSTER SYNDROME IS ESSENTIALLY THE OVERWHELMING AND CONSTANT FEELING OF 'I AM NOT GOOD ENOUGH', 'I DO NOT BELONG', OR 'THEY HAVE MADE A MISTAKE'.

I have experienced imposter syndrome about so many things at so many different times. Looking back to these moments, I truly wish I hadn't because I feel it would've made my time in those spaces much easier. A large chunk of the time I spent at Oxford was wasted on trying to convince myself that I was good enough. Despite believing I could do it *prior* to applying and telling myself I deserved nothing but the best that this world had to offer, once I was actually there the self-doubt kicked in. The biggest trigger for my imposter syndrome was not seeing people who looked or sounded like me, in a space that was so prestigious. So many people spoke about wanting to study there, so many tourists visited and paid insane amounts of money just to take a tour of a place where I was officially a student. Everyone around me sounded so different and had a completely different background to mine. Many had attended private schools and led extremely wealthy and privileged lives. There was also, of course, not only a lack of diversity in class and financial status but also in race. An overwhelming majority of the students at my university were white, while an extremely small minority were Black. Walking around and never seeing anyone who looked like me was what really made my imposter syndrome kick in. I began to doubt myself, wondering whether I was the 'right' type of student for a place like this.

Everyone else seemed so prepared, adjusting to Freshers' Week like it was nothing. We would attend things like formal dinners and there would be about five forks and knives either side of my plate. I'd watch the other students so effortlessly pick up the ones needed for each course while I sat there not knowing why we needed so many, let alone which one was for which course. We would attend afternoon teas or coffees and I would hear people talking about the 'horses' and the 'races' and how much they had enjoyed attending this one or that one because this happened or that happened. Meanwhile I had to secretly take my phone out to Google what 'the races' even were. I would sit in my Classical Archaeology and Ancient History group seminars and listen to the students and the teacher compare their favourite part of the popular Pyramids tour, while I mentally choked at the cost of a flight to Egypt. Things such as this played a huge role in enhancing the imposter syndrome I was already feeling. I began to wonder if the day would come when I'd be told that the admissions team had actually made a mistake and that I did not, in fact, belong at this institution. The feeling constantly played in my head during my first year of university. It infiltrated my dreams and kept me awake at night.

THE THING THAT BOTHERS ME MOST ABOUT IMPOSTER SYNDROME IS THAT IT HAPPENS TO THE PEOPLE WHO SHOULD FEEL IT THE LEAST. IT SADDENS ME WHEN I HEAR THOSE WHO HAVE TRULY WORKED HARD AND EARNED THEIR PLACE FEELING AS IF IT IS UNDESERVED, OR DOUBTING THEMSELVES, ESPECIALLY THE PEOPLE FROM LESS SUPPORTED AND LESS PRIVILEGED BACKGROUNDS.

These are the people who should feel proud of themselves; they managed to enter a position of privilege from a position of disadvantage. It makes the achievement that much more incredible.

This (and I wish Vee applying for Oxford knew this) should make you feel even more confident because it means you're capable, despite having the barriers that were previously in your way. It shows that you're innovative, can think of solutions and are able to adapt to whatever is needed. The very nature of coming from a lower socioeconomic background and managing to achieve what someone who is privileged has achieved shows the wealth of your abilities. Having to jump through hoops of fire to sit where you are sitting should exemplify how qualified and deserving you are. If anything, the person who had all the doors opened for them should feel more imposter syndrome. Who knows if they'd still be able to accomplish their goals if all that help was taken away from them? Securing a place, promotion or whatever goal it may be, is a testament to your ability, skill, and talent.

Reframing your anxieties

As I mentioned in the 'Rejection is Redirection' chapter, it's all about the framing of things. In this case, take what you feel insecure about and ask yourself, *why* do I feel inadequate here? Some of the questions that might be going through your head could be: 'Am I smart enough?', 'Do I belong?', 'Do I have enough experience?' If you take these worries and flip them on their head, they can be viewed positively.

When I was accepted into Harvard and worried about my lack of experience after the rejection of scholarships, etc., I had to reframe it. I was concerned that I had mistakenly been admitted to this prestigious university without having enough worldly experience in the field of education. My peers had either been teaching or in the education sector for ten-plus years and were extremely experienced. I had just received my undergraduate degree four months prior and was jumping straight into my Master's degree. This filled me with fear because I thought they would all view me as inadequate and that I wouldn't have anything to offer. However, a friend of mine encouraged me to see these anxieties from another perspective. That *despite* me not having worked in a role for ten-plus years in the education sector, I had *still* managed to secure a place at one of my dream universities on a competitive International Education Policy course. She reminded me that this showed just how talented and exceptional I was. She pointed out that I had still managed to work in the education community while doing a full-time undergraduate degree at an academically intense university. She allowed me to see how I had gotten creative and used social media to reach out to underrepresented communities, posting videos as a resource for others to use. How, when I couldn't yet get into classrooms to help students, I used my platform to mentor multiple students at the same time. How I had managed to champion girls' education in Zimbabwe while in England, since my degree didn't allow for me to take time off, etc. She said that it was this level of innovation that showed I cared and showed my desire to want to be a changemaker and eventually join the world leaders. The fact that I was completing a full-time degree was not going to stop me from doing the things I cared about. She said that it was this commitment to doing my part until I could be a qualified educator which got me into Harvard. She encouraged me in ways that I didn't know I needed and asked, 'Why not you?', 'Why can't you be one of the students that gains a place?' Any answer I tried to give she easily rebutted. Her unwavering confidence in me (and my own ability) kept me going and helped me fight off that imposter syndrome, but it wasn't easy, and even now I find it can come creeping back. The difference now is, the more I recognise it, the more I know how to deal with it. It took some time to understand where these emotions were coming from and eventually, I found a way of not only fighting the phenomenon, but also learning how to deal with it in a healthy and long-term way.

Reframing how I viewed my place, and seeing that I had more to offer than I had given myself credit for, helped boost my confidence in class. Instead of viewing myself as an under qualified twenty-two-year-old, I now saw myself as someone who had managed to do something despite having limited resources. Someone who had managed to create an online community of over 250,000 other students across the globe while getting a degree from one of her dream schools and fighting for equality and diversity within higher education for underrepresented students. I now took what I had achieved and focused on embracing that rather than fixating on what I had not *yet* gotten the chance to do. I think that a lot of us are often prone to doing this, writing ourselves off before we've even started. I'd already told myself that I wouldn't have anything to offer my peers before I'd even met them. I'm now one semester into my Harvard degree and can confirm that just as much as I'm learning from my peers, they're also learning from me. I find myself adding insightful information about global affairs from a student perspective using both my views and those of my audience. I find them turning to me to learn about Zimbabwean culture and politics, and how this intersects with the decisions made for girls' education.

I find myself becoming more and more instrumental in my classes and contributing to the shape of discussions and work. However, if I'd allowed my thoughts to take control, believing that I had nothing to add, I may have never applied or if I had, I may have never spoken in class out of fear.

Many people do this in the world of work. They never apply for the higher-paying job role because they think either they won't do the job well (despite having the skill set required), or that they aren't good enough and won't get it anyway, so why bother applying.

Many people do this in the world of work. They never apply for the higher-paying job role because they think either they won't do the job well (despite having the skill set required), or that they aren't good enough and won't get it anyway, so why bother applying. The issue with 'I won't get it anyway, so why bother applying?' is that it restricts you. It limits you to the options you think are available to you, to only ever doing the 'safe' things that you know you can get. The problem with this, as you can imagine, is that you may never get to be challenged, you may never get to maximise your skills or learn new ones and, worst of all, you may never get to live your dreams. If you allow your fear of 'not getting it anyway' to win, it means your fear comes true.

The irony of this mentality is that by virtue of never applying because you're afraid of not 'getting it', you'll never get it. The fear of the thing we want is bigger than what we have to do to get it. You are most likely to get that big promotion if you apply for it, but the fear of not getting it can become bigger than your desire. The actual task is simpler than the fear makes it. I always encourage people to apply, because the worst thing that can happen is that you don't get it, but in not getting it (as we mentioned in the 'Rejection is Redirection' chapter (see page 52) you may learn a lot about yourself and prepare yourself for something even greater. Not applying is never the answer because that doesn't help us advance or gain any information. If you apply and get the role, you will have elevated yourself, begun a new chapter and have the joy of gaining new skills in a new role. If you're not successful, you will learn what your strongest points are and which ones need some work. You can gain some practice in the interview process and build your confidence for the next time you try, or you might learn that that role was not quite right for you. But, by never applying you miss out on the unknown.

IT'S IMPORTANT IN YOUR SELF-EMPOWERMENT JOURNEY TO TAKE SOME RISKS.

This will sound very clichéd but high risk warrants high return. By fighting your imposter syndrome, you are investing in yourself. And, with self-investment there are always great returns. Taking the steps to overcome imposter syndrome will lead to you living a happier, more confident, and empowered life. Something that we all deserve. Imposter syndrome holds people back from truly exploring their passions, desires, or interests because of the fear of not being good enough. But the work of fighting or handling imposter syndrome is not an overnight job. It's still something that I manage now. Despite having proven my doubts wrong in almost all aspects of my life, it still somehow creeps in. It takes a lot of work, great practice, and consistent effort to keep it at bay.

The 'what will people think' phase

Something else that becomes an issue once you've overcome imposter syndrome is the 'what will people think' phase. Many people who feel undeserving of something will find it difficult to embrace their achievement not only internally, but also externally, because they worry about how they'll be viewed. This fear often comes from society having embedded stereotypes about people due to their sexuality, gender, race, and other factors; so much so that people feel the need to downplay their achievements or remain silent about them. It then becomes difficult to accept your achievements because you feel others around you think you undeserving. Fighting these negative comments, stereotypes, or the people trying to bring you down isn't easy. It makes me incredibly sad that you might have found happiness in an opportunity if someone hadn't said something negative to you. You may not have been insecure about it until someone else led you to think that way. We don't doubt ourselves or our position in the world until society tells us to. This type of imposter syndrome, the one that's been externally placed upon us, is often the hardest to undo. It takes more work because it requires not caring about what other people think, a task which is easier said than done. We live in a time when the opinion of others matters more than ever, especially on social media. Where photos, videos, and blog posts are judged on their quality based on how many people, literally, like it. This makes separating people's opinions from how we feel more difficult than it sounds.

My advice in these cases is that you must take control of your environment. It's important to choose good people to surround yourself with.

THOSE WHO ARE POSITIVE, WANT TO SEE YOU DO WELL AND WILL EVEN GO AS FAR AS HELPING YOU ACHIEVE YOUR LIFE GOALS. YOU NEED PEOPLE WHO SEE BEYOND THE EXTERIOR AND WHO DON'T DEFINE YOU SIMPLY BASED ON YOUR RACE, SEXUALITY OR GENDER. PEOPLE WHO TRY TO PLACE YOU IN A BOX AND TELL YOU WHAT YOU CAN AND CAN'T DO ARE NOT PEOPLE YOU NEED OR WANT TO BE AROUND. THESE PEOPLE WILL FEED INTO YOUR IMPOSTER SYNDROME AND PLAY A HUGE ROLE IN YOU 'NOT APPLYING' OR TRYING NEW THINGS.

Oftentimes their lack of support or lack of belief in you is typically a reflection of themselves. They might be afraid to go for their dreams and are intimidated when you are brave enough to do so, so they may try to bring you down with them. Therefore, it's crucial that you try to separate negative opinions from your own reality.

THE DIFFICULTY WITH TRYING TO SEPARATE PROJECTION FROM GENUINE ADVICE IS THAT YOU'LL INSTANTLY BELIEVE BOTH ARE TRUE.

Once we hear negative words, they are difficult to unhear. Black women and other marginalised groups are often *told* what they can and can't do, and often face rejection and dismissal from society based on their race. They are told they are aiming too high, that they are not good enough. They aren't represented in high-end campaigns, they're ignored by major make-up brands. They're copyrighted, manipulated, erased from history. All of this feeds directly into their subsequent imposter syndrome. These attitudes and more are embedded in our society and thus take a lot more work to undo. The treatment of Black women around the world and how much their abilities, beauty, and talent are judged and doubted truly breaks my heart. It means that instead of simply existing and enjoying our lives, we have to spend so much time undoing the work of those who oppress us. It's a deep shame that marginalised communities have to endure undoing the damage that they did not cause but rather was placed upon them. This is why I get so happy when I see Black and brown women succeeding and living their dreams because they really deserve it and more. Knowing that we deserve better is the first step. These negative opinions are a mixture of projections and things that have no business being given attention or thought. We cannot allow the deeply entrenched notion of imposter syndrome to win because if we do, it will, sadly, *always* win. We have to break these cycles and show the world we are *more* than the four walls they try to place us in.

Practical steps to Overcoming Imposter Syndrome

Before we get into the steps, I want to preface them by saying that overcoming imposter syndrome isn't something that will happen overnight. It's also not something that will magically vanish and never appear again. It's something you have to actively work at. It will be a constant work in progress and even after years of feeling great and not doubting your abilities, it will randomly crop up unexpectedly. What's important is to learn how to deal with it so that if it arises again, it doesn't win. Here are a few things you can do to practise:

1. Speak to yourself in the mirror. This is what I did while feeling overwhelmed by the culture at Oxford. I woke up every day and literally stood in front of the mirror and reminded myself of why I was worthy of having everything I had dreamed of. Constantly waking up and telling myself positive affirmations helped build my confidence. When you hear something so often you begin to believe it. I began to see myself in the same light as my family did. A kind, hardworking girl who was smart enough and good enough to be at one of her dream universities. *What are some positive affirmations you could say to yourself right now?*

   - 'I am good enough to be here'
   - 'my voice matters and it deserves to be heard'
   - 'it's okay not to be okay'
   - 'my ideas are worth sharing'
   - 'my best is good enough'

2. **Explore your feelings in a journal.** Whenever I felt doubt creeping in, I wrote in my diary. It was important for me to physically see what it was that I felt insecure or doubtful about. Once I had written a few words or a phrase in my diary, I would close the book and go to sleep or continue with my day. The next day, I would open it up and create a spider diagram around the words of doubt, writing down all the reasons why I shouldn't feel this way. Having spent time away from those feelings before coming to face them again helped me rationalise my thoughts. It allowed me to put things into perspective. Also, being able to break down how I felt on paper gave me the opportunity to spot the issues a lot more easily, so that I could address them with myself. Whenever I felt those emotions again, I could flick back to that diary entry and remind myself of the reasons why that imposter feeling was wrong.

3. **Turn to your support networks for guidance.** Something else that truly helped me fight my imposter syndrome, especially regarding my YouTube channel and putting myself on the internet, was (and still is) my older sister. Her unwavering confidence in me truly carried me through the negative thoughts when I wanted to give up. Putting myself out there for the world to see wasn't easy, and sometimes I'd be made fun of at university, but her 'ignore them' attitude helped me immensely. She's taught me about projection – how people try to put you down for the very things that they themselves feel insecure about or wish they were doing. Having someone like your sister, friend or partner being there, when you're feeling imposter syndrome, is extremely helpful. They can help you see that this is a self-doubt moment by reminding you of how incredible you are or offer you some constructive criticism.

4. **Know your triggers.** Try to acknowledge what it is that sends you into the 'I am not good enough' spiral. Try to remove those things from your space and build new habits. For so long I was insecure about my weight, something I don't ever talk about with people or on my social media platforms. I would find that the times I felt the worst about this were whenever I scrolled through my Instagram feed. I would see images of women who had undergone bodily enhancements as well as those who used photo-editing apps. I saw their bodies and wished I could look like them. This notion of 'not physically appearing good enough' would spiral into negative thoughts, and seep out into other aspects of my life. It would lead me to doubt my strength and willpower. If I couldn't easily lose weight and exercise self-control, then how could I be mentally fit enough to lead global change in education for young girls? I realise, looking back now, that the two notions don't correlate, but at the time it made complete sense to me. For this reason, I began to unfollow those unrealistic pages of photoshopped women. I realised that their presence in my space didn't serve me. Once I began to treat my social media space the same way I did my real life, filling it with things that were good, positive and informative for me, I began to feel better. If you can, it's essential that you try and find the source of your insecurity, the one that's feeding your imposter syndrome and try to get rid of or minimise it (if it's within your control).

WHAT ARE YOU WAITING FOR? LOOK YOUR IMPOSTER SYNDROME IN THE FACE AND TELL IT 'NOT TODAY MA'AM'.

Lean on Them

FORMING AN EMPOWERMENT CIRCLE

The top questions I receive on a daily basis are:

- **'Vee, how do you always remain so positive?'**
- **'Vee, how do you stay so happy all of the time?'**

Every time I hear these questions, I worry because I fear I may have portrayed something that isn't my reality. I'm not always happy, and I'm not always positive. There are many moments when I feel like giving up, many moments when I worry that things are not going to turn out well. These are the moments when I'm not okay, the moments when I struggle to take my own advice. The only way I get through these moments is by realising, as my sister always tells me, that 'it's okay not to be okay' and to 'lean on them'. Who is 'them'? And why is it okay not to be okay? Grab a cup of tea and let me explain.

THE ONLY WAY THAT I'VE BEEN ABLE TO SEE THOSE MOMENTS OF REJECTION AS REDIRECTION OR OVERCOME IMPOSTER SYNDROME IS BY HAVING MY EMPOWERMENT/ ACCOUNTABILITY CIRCLE AROUND ME. THESE ARE THE PEOPLE WHO REMIND ME TO DO MY POSITIVE AFFIRMATIONS, WHO ENCOURAGE ME TO TRY AGAIN AND TO FEEL EMPOWERED IN MY FAILURES.

They are the people who help me stay on top of my goals. It's all well and good to have an incredible goal list and to *know* that moments of failure are moments to try again, but it's a whole new level to *feel* these things as well. Your empowerment circle helps you implement the things you already know. You may know that this week you need to start putting aside £100 a week in order to reach that £400 per month goal to get to that £5,000 to achieve half of the house deposit by the end of the year; however, temptation is real and you are human. There will be moments when you *know* what is the right thing to do, but you fail to do it because life happens. Having your empowerment circle around you can help you remain on top of your A game, but they also help to hold you accountable by keeping you in check and ensuring you're keeping your promises to yourself.

One of the most effective empowerment or accountability groups I've ever seen has to be the one belonging to my friends George, James and Leon. I've never seen a group so dedicated to each other's success. They have phone calls about three times a week where they discuss at length how their goals are progressing and what they are struggling with. Having this group helps each of them do the things they said they would do and not allow any excuses – no matter how good they are – to get in the way. They check in on each other and try to address the barriers that are stopping them from doing what they set out to do. More often than not they find they have been unproductive due to distractions, stress or feeling overwhelmed. They've said that speaking these issues out loud, having people to share their wins and losses, really helps them process where they are in life and enjoy it, while also figuring out how to take the next steps.

> *Having accountability partners or empowerment groups helps you put a barrier between you, your excuses, and procrastination, because now there are other people watching and invested in your growth.*

As humans, we often have a way of talking ourselves out of the right thing to do, even if we know how important it is. We are also often victims of procrastination, knowing we have an essay due the next day but choosing to watch Netflix instead. Having accountability partners or empowerment groups helps you put a barrier between you, your excuses, and procrastination, because now there are other people watching and invested in your growth. My accountability and empowerment partners have been responsible for many of the successes I celebrate today. They've helped me reason when I'm feeling imposter syndrome. They encourage me to see my vision through a magnifying glass on a larger scale than I could've imagined. They help me see my talent and fight the self-doubt that often lurks in the back of my mind. My best friends (Malala and Josh) and my sister (Fadziee) are truly the greatest empowerment and accountability group I could've ever asked for. They are brutal in their honesty, but kind in their delivery. They are open to my new ideas but protective of how I present them. They want to see me shine brighter than any star in the universe but help keep me humble and grounded. The advice, guidance and love I've received from them is unmatched and has helped build me into the version of Vee whose book you are currently reading. Let me break down exactly what each of them does for me and why I call them my personal empowerment and accountability circle.

Malala's vision, experience and advice have taught me skills I never knew I lacked and opened me up to a world I didn't know existed. Every idea I present to her is taken with consideration, looked at from all angles, discussed at length and nurtured into fruition. She listens to me attentively, carefully points out the flaws in my plans and suggests different avenues that still help me arrive at the same destination. She encourages me to remember that life is a process and to take each moment for what it is and enjoy the small wins as they happen.

Joshua helps me reason. He helps me sit down and evaluate how each idea can be seen by the world, how it sounds in other rooms and how to adapt it. He helps make my ideas more versatile and gives them a scale beyond what I would've presented to him. He asks me the questions I don't want to hear, the ones that will make me go back and revamp the idea, the ones that make me do the work to ensure whatever I want to launch, present or discuss is in its best form. Joshua pushes me to think deeper and go beyond surface level, and to consider how the idea I have will look five years from now in various contexts. He brings me the clarity and reality I need to stand tall in any room with all the flaws in my projects addressed and fixed. Joshua is my sounding board and voice of reason.

My sister Fadziee is the beginning of it all. She's the one who helps me develop early ideas to fruition, the one who helps me turn the random thoughts in my mind into tangible ideas I can show the world. She's the creative in the family, the one who can turn dust into glitter. So much of what I do and how I present it has come from bouncing ideas back and forth with my sister in the late hours of the night. Many moments when I've wanted to give up, her guiding hand and encouraging voice have kept me going. Many moments when I've not wanted to acknowledge a win or saw it as a loss, she has lifted my spirits and helped me get back to focus mode. Having her keep me accountable and empowering me while I'm doing it has made me who I am today and for that I am forever grateful. She is the silent element of my loud production. She helps with every single thing that I do and I rely on her heavily for a lot of my ideas and my decisions. My sister taught me everything I know and in my journey of growth and self-love, she has been number one in providing the foundation for me seeing myself the way that I do now. I remember writing her a song when I was fourteen years old detailing how much she meant to me, and how she had helped me find my wings so that I could fly. She shows me that being assertive does not necessarily make you a bad person; rather it makes you a person who knows how to communicate their discomfort and do so effectively. Having the open and honest relationship that I have with my sister means everything to me. I get to lean on her, and enjoy constantly doing life with my best friend.

Our relationship was not always like this. We were not always close and I'm pretty sure that gap was created due to our separation when we were younger. The initial bonding that should've come with those early years was taken away. We had to learn, really learn, to love one another and also to hear each other. Fadziee is one of those people who when they love, they love hard. She makes it work, always, no matter what; even if it's my birthday and she doesn't have a lot of money, she will find ways to make me feel special by making our favourite dishes from our favourite restaurants. There have been times in our lives when people try to compare us and ask my sister why she is not performing at the same pace as me or anything along these lines; my heart genuinely breaks. My sister and I have overcome so much, and both choose to live life at the pace that suits us while doing the things that we enjoy. She is making her mark in the world in the way she wants to and using her own means. Having people make these comments to us when growing up thankfully drew us closer. We stand up to each person and correct them, letting them know that we are on different journeys with different destinations and that is the beauty of life: you can be a unit but also be individuals within it.

My sister essentially allowed me to practise my 'saying no' and my 'you're overstepping the boundary' facial expressions. She's helped me navigate how to own what I am doing and what I have done. Her love knows no bounds when it comes to her younger sister and I will forever be grateful for her guiding hand hyping me up as I navigate this thing called life. So, if you have a friend or cousin, or someone whom you're extremely close to and trust with all of your heart, ask them if you can use them as a sounding board. Let them hear your thoughts and help you articulate and present them better. This person has to be someone who is not afraid of being completely honest with you. They must be okay with helping you step out of your comfort zone. You want people around you who want to challenge you and help you grow, so much so that when you come to them with an idea, they will say, 'How will it work and what do you need?' instead of 'What's the point of what you're doing, don't do it'. These types of people are the ones who are not invested in you, what you do or what will be your legacy!

THIS IS THE IMPORTANCE OF GROWTH IN YOUR LIFE AND OF MAINTAINING CONTROL OF YOUR DECISIONS, IT'S THE ART OF KNOWING WHAT YOU NEED AND WHEN YOU NEED IT.

Right now, in my life, I do not want to hear people tell me that they 'love me just the way I am' because I am coming to them for advice on how to elevate, and those words are not what I want to hear. I want to be the best version of myself; I want to create generational wealth for my future children; I want to help create generational change within the education system for girls around the world; I want to help lead policy reform and do so much more. What I do not want is to be told to remain just as I am because that version of Vee does not grow and that version of Vee becomes too comfortable, and you know one of my top rules is to start becoming uncomfortable with being too comfortable. You want to push yourself and have people around you who do the same. Having my sister as a sounding board and someone I know I can always count on no matter what is incredible. It settles me, puts me at ease and reminds me that despite the outcome of my ideas, my accomplishments or accolades, my sister still appreciates me for the woman I am becoming; a young, confident and ambitious girl who cares about the world and the people in it. It helps me lose the fear of taking risks, of exploring new ideas and of putting myself out there, because my sister inspires me to stand in my power and believe in myself.

Essentially, there will be no move made or idea presented to the world that I don't run by those three people. They keep me grounded and help me keep it moving. They also help me realise that it's okay not to be okay and *allow* me not to be okay. Not for a long time of course, but enough that I can process my emotions, grieve whatever I'm feeling a loss for and acknowledge that that feeling existed. Because of my 'happy-go-lucky' attitude towards life, I fear that people may think I'm saying you should never be sad. This isn't the case. I'm saying that you should definitely acknowledge those moments of pain, sadness and anger, it's part of the growth process and part of being human. We experience a range of emotions and that's okay. What makes you strong is what you do with these feelings once you've acknowledged them.

How do you then turn them into something positive that you have control over? Typically, when something bad occurs that upsets me or makes me feel angry, my friends and family leave me to it for a day or two. They allow me to wallow and feel whatever I feel. Unfortunately, I can't recommend a time frame for how long you should experience these emotions because everyone is different and has a different healing process, so please listen to your body, mental health, and general energy. For me, however, two days is enough.

IT'S OKAY TO SAY YOU GOT TO WHERE YOU ARE WITH THE HELP OF THOSE AROUND YOU. IT DOESN'T TAKE AWAY FROM YOUR ACHIEVEMENT. IT JUST MEANS YOU LEANED INTO THOSE AROUND YOU WHO BELIEVED IN YOUR VISION.

My accountability circle allows me to sit, think and be at one with my emotions and then, when adequate time has passed, they remind me of all the things I mentioned in the previous chapters. They'll tell me that rejection is redirection, that I can readjust my goals to fit my new context, that I'm deserving of the job offer I've just received and that my imposter syndrome is nothing but fear that's trying to take control over my mind. They remind me of all the things I want and what sober-minded Vee would say right now if her mind wasn't clouded with emotion. They essentially help me bounce back and lean on them. I often hate how single minded we've become in our generation and how we really glamourise the struggle. In my mind, those who have struggled have the ability to overcome difficult situations and persevere, but where you don't have to struggle or even be alone, you don't have to. It's okay to say you got to where you are with the help of those around you. It doesn't take away from your achievement. It just means you leaned into those around you who believed in your vision. This is a good thing and I strongly encourage it, especially if you're running a business or a network group, etc. – delegation and having a team will save you so much time and allow for you to do the things that matter most to you. Allow someone who is willing and able to take over the things that you may not be so good at, such as admin or finances. This will give you space to focus on your strengths and the things that really need your attention. Here comes another cliché that's so true that it hurts, but 'a problem shared is a problem halved'. Having this accountability and empowerment group present in your life makes any and all problems easier to handle.

The power of the word 'no'

Something else that my empowerment circle did was teach me the power of the word 'no'. For so long I allowed people to tell me what to do, what to feel and how to be. There were times when people would try and take advantage of me. I wouldn't be able to see the situation clearly but my sister or Josh would realise and help me get out of the situation before it was too late. Many of these people wanted to control the things I had achieved and use the platforms I had created as their own. Out of guilt at appearing selfish or out of touch, I always said yes. I said yes so much that my weekends were spent simply fulfilling the wishes and demands of others. I had no time for myself and ended up feeling exhausted and resentful of those who were asking so much of me. It wasn't until I learned to say the word 'no' that I felt alive and empowered within my assertiveness.

YOU MUST REMEMBER TO PROTECT YOUR SPACE, TIME AND ENERGY. AGAIN, THIS IS A GENTLE REMINDER THAT YOU DON'T HAVE TO WALK THROUGH LIFE ALONE AND THAT IT'S IMPORTANT TO HAVE THE RIGHT COMMUNITY BEHIND YOU. LEAN ON THEM!

I assess the consequences for myself if I were to carry out the favour, the consequences for the person asking, if I couldn't do what they needed, and the general damage it could do to our relationship. When I began to think this way, I filtered through many of the requests with ease. Nine times out of ten, the people could fulfil their request themselves. It would take them a little bit longer, but they came to me because they wanted a fast track for their query or problem. Most of the time the things they were asking for or about could easily be solved by a simple Google search. You must remember to protect your space, time and energy. Again, this is a gentle reminder that you don't have to walk through life alone and that it's important to have the right community behind you. Lean on them!

Nine times out of ten, the people could fulfil their request themselves. It would take them a little bit longer, but they came to me because they wanted a fast track for their query or problem.

Find people who motivate you

Another reason why I love my empowerment circle and my wider group of friends is because they all motivate me. I'm lucky enough to say that I don't have to look far for inspiration because it's constantly around me. Any time I open my phone to check updates or just to browse social media, I see my friends doing incredible things all year round. They are all so young, so passionate, and so driven and it drives me to be the best version of myself. They are my biggest inspirations. I wouldn't be able to visualise my own potential without the knowledge of their own achievements. I appreciate my circle now more than ever probably because I grew up with a lack of role models and goals to aspire to. I've seen what can happen when you're told there's a limit to what you can do. When your teachers focus on you simply passing, you go through life doing just that, *passing*. Having friends around me who always see the bigger picture, who have a 'can-do' attitude is phenomenal, and if you have people within your reach who make you feel motivated and ready to go, keep them around you!

I remember applying to Harvard and feeling nervous and out of my depth. Despite having attended Oxford and being on track to get a good grade, I still felt an overwhelming sense of imposter syndrome. I just kept wondering, *what if I'm not experienced enough, what if there are students better than I am? What if I fail the admissions test and they realise I'm not smart enough?* I worried about sitting in a university with future leaders and those who were going to change the world, and feeling inadequate. I was anxious about their greatness reflecting on my lack thereof. So many emotions were running through my mind as I was applying and there were many moments when I almost gave up. I was stuck between a rock and a hard place, because I didn't want to tell anyone in case I drew too much attention to myself and put pressure on the process and the outcome. However, I wanted guidance so that it felt less daunting. When I'd exhausted every YouTube video on how to apply, how to ace the interview, etc., I summoned up the courage to reach out to someone I'd always admired from a distance. I got in touch with the former African and Caribbean Society President at Oxford University, Renee Kapuku. We had been at university for our undergraduate degrees but she was two years above me. I had found her leadership incredibly graceful but powerful, and was in awe of how she could silence a room with her soft-spoken voice while simultaneously keeping it energised. Whenever I heard her speak or give a talk to the group, I'd mentally take notes and wish that one day I could navigate life in such an assertive and unapologetic way. When she graduated, we connected more through social media and I finally let her know what a profound impact she had had on my time at Oxford without us ever having had a real or lengthy conversation. Our friendship blossomed and ever since then, I've looked to her as a mentor, sister, and friend that I hope to have for life.

After Renee had graduated with a jaw-dropping first-class degree from Oxford University, she had gone on to study her Master's degree at Harvard on a fully funded scholarship. Thus, when it came time for me to apply, it was a no brainer for me to reach out to her for advice. I cannot stress this enough, but the reception I received from Renee and her response to my fears and questions is possibly one of the top reasons why I ended up applying. She didn't hesitate when she spoke about how much confidence she had in me and my abilities. She said I was more capable of doing this than I thought and that the only thing that would lessen my chances was if I did *not* apply. I mentioned to her in passing that I wanted to come and visit

Harvard just so I could see it and make it more real in my mind, and without hesitation dates were arranged. Within a few months, I was on campus and she was showing me around. She made something that felt so unattainable in my mind feel like it was as simple as a walk in the park. She told me what books she had read to prepare for the entrance exams, showed me which YouTube videos to watch, and let me pick her brain day and night until I was comfortable and the application process was over. Renee's willingness to support me in any way that she could helped me overcome my imposter syndrome. She allowed me to believe in myself and I will never forget this.

It's important to recognise these people and give them credit where it's due. I have a rule with myself now that whenever I see anyone doing something I like or enjoy or have benefited from, I immediately send them a message to let them know.

Having someone like Renee in my life uplifted me and showed me the power of speaking things into existence. There's power in preparing for what you want and becoming relentless in pursuing it. If you can become that for someone or know someone in your life who motivates you in this way, reach out to them, let them know what their work (whether it be blog posts, tweets, etc.) is doing for you or has done for you. It's important to recognise these people and give them credit where it's due. I have a rule with myself now that whenever I see anyone doing something I like or enjoy or have benefited from, I immediately send them a message to let them know. I think often we consume people's content, words, or stories, gain from them, and never let them know how widespread their impact has been. Renee has been one of my biggest inspirations for the past few years. The woman I am growing into today is because of her, and despite how much I tell her, she will never truly understand the depth of the impact she has had on me. We have now built a sisterhood where we support each other in any way that we can, when we can. Whenever I see her videos, blog posts or podcast updates, I share them with my audience because I know so many will gain value from what she has to say. Renee and I check in on each other's mental health, emotions, and wellbeing too. She's one of the few people to ask, 'But Vee, really, how are *you*?' instead of just asking how things with work, etc. are going. For that, and so much more, I appreciate her. These relationships have to be mutual, enjoyable and genuine. They cannot be one sided otherwise you risk draining the other person or people in your life.

SO, ALWAYS ASK YOURSELF, HOW CAN I ALSO ADD VALUE TO THE PERSON WHO SUPPORTS ME SO MUCH? HOW CAN I SUPPORT THEM OR SIMPLY JUST BE A SOURCE FOR THEM TO BOUNCE IDEAS OFF, OR COME TO WHEN THEY NEED TO SPEAK?

Choosing your empowerment circle wisely

Your friends, family, and colleagues can become some of the biggest sources of inspiration in your lives, so lean on them. As mentioned, my sister Fadziee is someone who has taught me the art of self-confidence. For so long I wanted to downplay my achievements out of fear of making others feel inadequate. I always feared that some of the things I had had the opportunity to do or achieve were anomalies and thus shouting about them would be insensitive to others my age. My sister is the one who shook this thinking out of my system. She told me that my reasons for sharing my story have always been, and will always be, for the sake of helping others. She reminded me of something I previously told her – that I never wanted to hold back any information I had learned that could help others gain access to opportunities. She insisted I become unapologetic in the spaces that I enter because my presence would make room for other young Black girls in the future. When I began to view things from this angle, I became unstoppable in how I shared my story online. I shouted about the things I had learned, the brands I had worked with, the schools I had attended, the people I had met and the things I had seen. I wanted other young people to know it was possible, that the only thing a lot of us lacked was access and information.

The young people I've met since I began advocating for access to education truly inspire me. They're some of the most talented, intelligent and incredible human beings. They're ten steps ahead in their innovation, creativity, and potential; however, by virtue of where many of them were born or their household income, or where they attended school, they're unable to access incredible opportunities. These people repeatedly demonstrate how capable they are but are never given a chance. Seeing this type of inequality among many of

YOUR FRIENDS, FAMILY, AND COLLEAGUES CAN BECOME SOME OF THE BIGGEST SOURCES OF INSPIRATION IN YOUR LIVES, SO LEAN ON THEM.

my peers or those from areas like mine is what pushed me even further to start sharing tips and advice online to large groups of people. I wanted to help break the secret circles and bring the conversations to everyone. It was from this that my YouTube channel was born, but this couldn't have happened without the relentless encouragement of my sister and my mother.

My point is, many of the opportunities I've had have come from friends of friends recommending me, my sister pushing me, or my best friends helping me to develop weak ideas into strong and powerful ones. Nothing I've done in the past few years has been done alone. It's been through the help and strength of my circle. There's a saying that goes, 'You are an average of the five closest people to you,' and the older I get the more I see it. The people I surround myself with allow me to be my true and authentic self. They allow me to grow, develop and push myself beyond what I think I'm capable of. They help me to see myself through their eyes, a perspective that's so different to my own perception of myself. So, when you have the chance, sit down and look around you. Ask yourself, who have I put my trust into enough that I have let them into my circle, into my space? The people you are close to have access to your energy. They have the ability to help you see the world in a certain way.

If you surround yourself with people who genuinely hate life, it's not surprising if you constantly have a low energy when you're around them. When the people around you have a desire to live their lives to the fullest, to make the best out of bad situations and to reframe things that may have been out of their control, there's a high chance you will begin to do the same. It's difficult to be angry in a room full of happy people or to be negative around those who see the brighter side of life. Ask yourself, who are you spending many hours of your day with? How are you both serving each other in your journeys to empowerment and living a happier and more productive life? Look in the mirror to see the role you are playing in other people's lives. Self-awareness is one of the greatest tools one can have. Read your own body language, the way you speak to others. Are you bringing people down? Are you a helpful person in your friendships? Are you dismissive when your friends approach you? If you carry negative traits and are passing on bad energy to others, you should sit down and evaluate why. Before you can be of help to others or expect help from them, you must be sure that you are also bringing something to their tables. When choosing your circle of friends, choose them wisely and choose them authentically.

Before you can be of help to others or expect help from them, you must be sure that you are also bringing something to their tables. When choosing your circle of friends, choose them wisely and choose them authentically.

If you feel there are any relationships that are holding you back, are toxic or make you feel less than, cut them off! If you notice yourself having to downplay things in order to not hurt someone else's feelings – not because they're in a bad place but because they're *always* like this . . . if you notice that they seem happier to be around you when you're feeling low or that they always remind you of the negative when discussing ways to advance your life . . . if being with them fills your mind with doubt or constantly makes you feel uneasy . . . then you're probably in an unhealthy or toxic relationship. One of the biggest life lessons you will learn is how to let these relationships go. It feels easier said than done, but it's important to know when to cut your losses and accept that something is just not working.

How do you do this, I hear you ask? It all comes from a simple conversation. Let them know about certain behaviours you've noticed and how they are affecting you. Their response will speak volumes. They will either want to fix things or tell you your feelings are invalid. If you feel you've been dismissed and the behaviour does not change, then it's time for you to move on. Explain that you need space or are done with the friendship and stop responding to their lines of communication. This is to protect your own state of mind. Your future self will thank you for it and you'll find yourself less stressed. You have to limit your exposure to toxic people. You deserve to live a happy life, and having anyone who is intentionally in the way of that process will be unhealthy not only for you, but also for the person in question. Cutting anyone off will be one of the most emotionally tasking things you'll have to do, but the most rewarding for your progress and development. If the people in your circle are not pushing you to aim higher, you do not have a circle, you have a cage. This is YOUR life and those around you will influence and shape that, so where you can, take control, and fill your space with positive and genuine people that will help push you, love you, and support you.

An inspiring podcast to listen to

As if I haven't sung Renee's praises enough, her 'To My Sisters' podcast, which she co-hosts with her best friend, Courtney Daniella, is phenomenal. I don't know how else to describe it. It has changed my mindset and has helped me understand life from a new perspective. It does exactly what it says on the tin, addresses women all over the world about issues that we experience but never get to talk about aloud or in such a nuanced way. The podcast covers everything from finances, sex, faith, academia, activism, love and more. The breadth of topics discussed represents the multifaceted lives we lead as women. It shows how intersectionality works and exemplifies how two things can be true at the same time. For example, you can be both Black and rich or Christian and hypersexual. They help remind us of how multifaceted women are and their endless layers; in my mind they are breaking down these stereotypes, one podcast episode at a time. I love how in-depth their discussions are, helping me to see a perspective to an issue that I had never considered.

The podcast is the embodiment of my relationship with Renee. It demonstrates her wisdom when giving advice, and shows that she can be both a fountain of knowledge and out of her depth when a subject is beyond her. I love how she's aware of herself, her past, her flaws, her strengths, and how she can serve in this world. The way that she and Courtney bounce off each other is beautiful and makes the listener feel like they are at lunch with their sisters and just having a general chat. That is one of the main reasons why I'm obsessed with the podcast; it manages to provide an element of intimacy and personalisation despite it being heard by thousands of people. I love the community that they are building around it too, with many people like myself swearing we wish we'd had something like this while growing up. Something about their raw and unapologetic honesty makes you feel seen and heard. I typically listen to them during my daily walks as it helps me focus on something positive and gives me time to digest what they're saying. The podcast has helped me feel empowered in my femininity, my stance on certain things like dating, roles within relationships and more. I would highly recommend this listen to those feeling slightly lost, and those in need of a deep, intellectual, and understanding conversation about life.

Practical steps to maintaining your empowerment circle

- Do they check in on you and ask you how you genuinely feel?
- Do they make you feel encouraged?
- If you hear good news, would you want to tell them as soon as you could?
- Do you feel comfortable in sharing your failures with them?
- Do you feel safe sharing your dream goals with them?
- If you created a product, would you be happy to let them see it before the world does?

These questions really help you gauge who you naturally lean on and perhaps these are the people who have been part of your empowerment circle all along. Allow people to be there for you because it really does take a village to nurture someone. We are not built to navigate life on our own, so why suffer? One of the best investments you can have is mentorship and a healthy network. Your network, as they say, is your net worth. You need to ensure you're getting advice from the right people. Those who've walked in your shoes before and are in that future position you would aspire to. Pick their brains and gain insight into their minds. There's nothing more powerful or resourceful than being able to gain access into the tips and tricks of a successful person. They'll tell you about their wins and failures, from which you can learn a lot. If you can't gain this kind of access, that's okay – you can still have a similar experience by reading or listening to content about these people's lives. You can learn more about how they got to where they are, and how they overcame the fear of starting whatever it is that they do. Hearing these kinds of conversations and thoughts will help you see your journey in a new light. It will show you that it's important to keep pushing because eventually it will pay off and give you a source of inspiration.

Ensure that as much as you get from these people, you are also giving back to them. Whenever I feel like something I am doing came directly from Renee's guidance, I make sure to let her know. I thank her for what she provides for me: a safe space to be my true and authentic self. I send her random gifts or make sure I include her in the things I have going on, not only because I want to show my deep appreciation for her support, but mainly because she is great at what she does. She is one of the wisest people I have ever met. Her advice and input are invaluable, so I support her to the best of my ability. I once heard this saying that stuck with me, 'Give them their flowers while they are still here.' I have noticed that it's not until someone is no longer with us that people express their deepest gratitude. I do not want that to be me. I want to give everyone their credit and dues while they are still here. If you can give your empowerment circle their metaphorical (or physical) flowers now, do it, so they can enjoy them.

Me, Myself and Social Media

HOW TO EMPOWER YOURSELF
WHILE SURVIVING SOCIAL MEDIA

SOCIAL MEDIA. The space that allows us to

connect with our loved ones, share our lives with strangers, keep up with those we find inspirational and create business ventures. Social media is a tool that has allowed those doing meaningful work to spread their message far and wide, and touch the lives of those they would otherwise have not had access to. Equally, it is the space that allows those who have hatred in their hearts to spread harmful speech that can destroy the lives of many.

It is safe to say that I have a love–hate relationship with social media. This is something I went into depth about when I was invited to a recorded conversation with the Duke and Duchess of Sussex, Harry and Meghan. I had been invited to the talk by the Queen's Commonwealth Trust charity organisation, where a few changemakers were asked to have a productive conversation with Harry and Meghan to bring light to the dangers of social media. Our conversation centred around how to use social networks as a tool for good and create positive changes for young people on the internet. We spoke about how, when used for good, social media can truly change lives while also creating safe and productive spaces for those seeking to be heard and be part of a community. The discussion helped me see how much more work needed to be done, and hearing Meghan, someone I find so inspirational and brave, tell me that the work I was doing was needed in the world, was extremely uplifting and encouraging.

SOCIAL MEDIA HAS ALLOWED ME TO TAKE MY PASSION AND TIMES IT BY TEN. IT HAS ALLOWED ME TO CONNECT WITH PEOPLE WHO ARE LIKE-MINDED, PEOPLE WHO, LIKE ME, WANT TO SEE THE WORLD BECOME A BETTER PLACE.

It has given me the chance of having my voice heard by hundreds of thousands of people, and access to resources I could only ever dream of. Following the horrific death of George Floyd in the USA, I was feeling extremely angry at what some world leaders were saying, as well as various groups on social media. I wanted to get my voice heard and to try and educate those who were spreading false truths. I recorded a video titled 'Why Black people are tired and angry' to bust the myths that were circulating on the internet. In the video, I spoke about the history of oppression against Black people, and how police brutality plays a part in this. I told the viewers that Black people were angry because these were not one-off events, these were not accidents, rather these acts of violence were consistent, and our anger stemmed from such acts going unpunished and unchecked. I made sure I spoke about police brutality and racism from the British perspective too, as I felt it was something often not discussed. The magnifying glass seemed to be on the United States only. I recommended books that people could read to help educate themselves. This video received over 200,000 views and was circulated in the YouTube newsletter as a must-watch educational piece of content. In this case, social media helped me contribute to the Black Lives Matter conversation and reach many people in the UK and beyond, allowing me to discuss a topic that was close to my heart.

SOCIAL MEDIA HAS ALSO TORN ME DOWN.

It has made me want to (metaphorically) bury my head in the sand. I am aware that no matter what you do, some people will always have something negative to say. What frustrates me is not necessarily the fact that someone has said something unkind, but that some of these people attach themselves to me and my work. These people avidly follow me, check in on everything that I do, take it back to a hate forum and discuss it at length. I cannot for the life of me understand why. There have been a few times in my life when I have not liked someone's content or what they stood for. Do you know what I did? I simply unfollowed them and refused to support their content or add to their community. This is what I feel everyone should do when they find someone annoying, especially when it is based on a personal opinion about things that are outside the creator's control, such as their dress sense or appearance.

Another aspect of social media that stresses me out is the one that causes young girls to feel insecure. As mentioned above, I wish everyone would remove pages and accounts that cause them stress from their feeds and social media as a whole. There is genuinely nobody on Instagram that I follow but secretly dislike or feel triggered by. I feel that it would be damaging to my mental health if every time I was browsing the net, I was bombarded with things that caused me to feel low.

There are definite hurdles and learning opportunities to be had with social media. It teaches you very quickly how to deal with the demands of an online public, which has made me very good at putting up healthy boundaries. I have had to learn to honour my time, energy and mental health. It took some time to get there, and in the beginning, I remember trying to reply to every single message I received. I wanted to be there for everyone as I was extremely grateful to have their support. I also had a deep desire to just help in any way I could. However, this became exhausting very quickly and I realised it was not sustainable. At minimum and on a daily basis, I may receive at least 100 messages between Instagram, Twitter, LinkedIn and email. The messages are usually lengthy with specific requests for help with academic work, advice or financial support. As you can see, it would be impossible to reply to every message, as my days would be spent replying instead of producing helpful content, studying and my other activities. I realised that my desire to reply would not work on a long-term basis as I would want to give adequate attention to every question. I also realised I couldn't do this while juggling a full-time education. I decided to find alternative methods where I could still interact with people. I began using methods such as public Q&As where I could answer a person's question publicly and thus help others who may have had the same question. This worked out far better than doing constant individual replies. I had to draw this boundary early on, as I was finding myself tired the majority of the time and unable to keep up with

There are definite hurdles and learning opportunities to be had with social media. It teaches you very quickly how to deal with the demands of an online public, which has made me very good at putting up healthy boundaries. I have had to learn to honour my time, energy and mental health.

my university work and other daily commitments. Putting up the necessary boundaries ensured that I could stay on top of my work but also still do what I love and create content for my community.

Get comfortable with being uncomfortable

One of the key takeaways I've learned about my online work is that, in order to serve others, it's important to be at your best. If you're not feeling 100 per cent, it's difficult to see how you can perform at your best, especially if you're navigating a world where you serve others like I do. If you're currently low, dig deep and do the things that can help you deal with this feeling. For me, my time is dedicated largely to interacting with a wide audience. My days consist of giving advice, providing resources, and helping with access to education. This means that I need to be at my best because people *depend* on my best. I am of no help to my students if I have not taken care of myself. But, to take on roles like this, it's mandatory that you take care of *you* first, before you can take care of anyone else. This is the time that you need to focus on building you. Building you is the most important part of this journey. The foundations and the roots must be laid down before you try to water them. Essentially, you need to show up and show out for yourself and *make* yourself uncomfortable. What do I mean by this? You already know the drill people, grab a cup of tea, sit back, and make some notes!

One of the best things you could ever do for yourself is to become comfortable with being uncomfortable, in order to live up to your dreams.

YOU HAVE TO TAKE RISKS AND INVEST IN YOUR GOALS AND ASPIRATIONS. DO NOT LET SOCIAL MEDIA TELL YOU WHO YOU ARE OR WHAT YOU'RE SUPPOSED TO ACHIEVE.

You can lose yourself trying to please people on social media who you may never meet in your real life. The opinions of strangers can seriously impact us, and it is human nature to zoom in on them, but truthfully, they shouldn't matter. If you're aspiring to apply for your dream university, become a musician, become a model or whatever it may be, you have to go ten times harder at everything you do. Start to invest in yourself and ignore the outside world. It might take you extra time to practise your entrance exam many months prior to the test coming up, or playing music in the street to strangers to get feedback on your songs while waiting to be discovered. Investing in yourself might mean using the pavement near your street to practise walking down the catwalk before you ever get a chance to be on stage. What I'm saying here is that you need to ask yourself, what am I doing to prepare for my future and my desires? How am I investing in myself daily? It is really important to know what you want and if the things you consume on social media are helping towards your mental health or encouraging you constructively.

You need to ask yourself, what am I doing to prepare for my future and my desires? How am I investing in myself daily? It is really important to know what you want and if the things you consume on social media are helping towards your mental health or encouraging you constructively.

As we know, 'with high risk comes high reward'. The more you give, the more you get. Start using social media for scouting out other people who are doing what you're doing or killing it in your lane so that you know what's at stake. Do small things like reading more books or watching YouTube videos on the subject you're interested in. The only way to get good at something is to practise it over and over again until you become an expert.

You want the world to say, 'We need _____ because they're the expert in _____.' Choose your area, choose your subject (for *now*, not forever, as we are constantly evolving and so are our interests) and progress with the aim of becoming a trusted and reliable voice in it. Create a demand for what you want to provide the world with and supply it. If your goals don't scare you, then they just aren't big enough. They should excite you and make you want to get out of your comfort zone. They should make you want to innovate, grow, and create.

Remember that this can look different for everyone. One person's version of a dream goal is another person's worst nightmare. One person's nightmare is someone else's dream goal. Just remember to take everything I say and apply it to *you* and *your* dreams.

Learn how to re-engage with social media

Social media can set unrealistic standards for young people and lead them to believe that things can happen overnight. I know that there are exceptions to this rule, but typically, you have to work at something for a long time before you see results. People need to trust you, no matter what you're doing. You must also be consistent in what you're doing to show that you're reliable. The thing with social media is that people only show you the highlights, the 'ups' of their journey and the moments of winning. What you don't get to see is the behind the scenes, the 'getting there' moments. In today's social media age, we have unlimited access to other peoples' lives. Within one click, we know what our favourite celebrities, family members and friends are wearing, eating, buying, and achieving. Whilst the last one doesn't sound dangerous, having an endless stream of this can lead us to set unrealistic standards for what we should physically look like, how we should speak and what we should have accomplished by a certain age. For many young people, the notion of success is based on someone else's reality, which means that the standards being set are, in many cases, unattainable. Like the face-tuned and photoshopped pictures we see and attribute to 'natural beauty', when we see people standing in front of their new houses and cars, we assume these to be 'authentic'. However, social media doesn't tell the full story – it gives us the highlights without the context, so it's important to remember that these things don't happen at the click of a finger.

A phenomenal friend of mine, Hayley Mulenda, once posted a picture of herself on Twitter speaking to thousands of people at Wembley Stadium. The picture gained a lot of traction with thousands retweeting and commenting. Many people left comments expressing their desire to be her and how they wished they could speak in front of that many people. Because of Hayley's age, many people began comparing themselves to her, saying that they wished they were at her stage now. True to her character, Hayley quickly corrected everyone, telling them not to wish for something they didn't fully understand or even know about. She explained that everyone was seeing a picture of her success but they wouldn't believe the journey she had to walk to stand on that stage. She shared her many rejections and moments of depression, revealing how she once wanted to end her pain by taking her own life. She encouraged her followers to appreciate their own journey, wherever they were currently in their lives. She prompted her followers not to allow social media to rush them because, quite literally, people never paint the full picture. Hayley's openness and rawness are two of the many reasons I admire her. I wish more figures in society would help to remove the rose-tinted filters creating unrealistic expectations.

Social media has become our space to escape and has provided the chance to gain insight into the lives of our peers and those that we admire. If used wisely, it can be an incredible resource to empower you. You can curate your feed into whatever you want based on the people you follow. I generally enjoy content about education, lifestyle, and empowerment. My social media is my safe space to explore what those around me are doing and use as a source of inspiration. Once upon a time, I felt extremely insecure about my appearance and worried I wasn't evolving or developing at the same pace as my peers in terms of fashion, physical appearance, and having the general 'look'. I enjoyed wearing my natural hair in a ponytail and throwing on dungarees and a backpack. Just picture a Dora the Explorer vibe but in human form. But I always did feel a little left out because I never knew or understood what was on trend and thus could not join into the conversations with my

SOCIAL MEDIA HAS BECOME OUR SPACE TO ESCAPE AND HAS PROVIDED THE CHANCE TO GAIN INSIGHT INTO THE LIVES OF OUR PEERS AND THOSE THAT WE ADMIRE. IF USED WISELY, IT CAN BE AN INCREDIBLE RESOURCE TO EMPOWER YOU.

sister and friends. I did try to fit in and do what my peers were doing but it didn't feel like me. I was trying to dress in a way that was not comfortable for me. It looked beautiful on those around me but didn't feel right for me. I was essentially trying to keep up with a lifestyle that wasn't mine and it became extremely time consuming and costly. I was spending longer in the mornings trying to choose outfits; I was becoming late for meetings and events. I worried about how I would sleep in case I messed up my wig or how to avoid breaking out in spots because I was now wearing makeup seven days a week for long hours. I just couldn't sustain this high-maintenance lifestyle and ultimately went back to my simplistic ways. I told myself that the time would come when I'd naturally gravitate towards hair, makeup and dressing up but now just wasn't it. I learned how to become comfortable in my own skin, as well as owning what I enjoyed and what I did *not* enjoy. For so long I was afraid that not liking or even 'getting' some of the things my peers were into made me uncool. I felt as if I were missing out. Why hadn't it clicked for me the same way it had for my peers? It dawned on me later that we all have our timings.

Essentially, you have to focus on your own talents and your own way of doing things. Trust your timing. You're here to make things happen for you and to be in control of your destiny. Don't allow that Instagram picture of the twenty-one-year-old who just purchased a house to rush you. Don't allow that picture to put pressure on you or make you feel like you need to put yourself in debt just so that you can also buy a house. Don't give control of your life over to someone you don't know and who doesn't know you! It's like trusting a stranger you just met on the street with your baby for an entire night without telling them the baby's feeding hours, their allergies, or even their name, all the while hoping that the stranger will do a good job of keeping your child safe. The person in the picture that you might be allowing to control you doesn't know your journey, struggle, or hardships, your strengths or weaknesses. How can you then let pictures set the standard for your own reality? Don't do it! Use them for inspiration, use them to enjoy seeing other people doing well, but don't use them to rush yourself or force yourself into a lifestyle you're not yet ready to maintain.

So many of us are afraid of the journey, of failing, of looking silly, so we give up before we even begin. We use social media as our basis for what's okay to do and not to do so much that we may never bring out our own ideas. We also fear that it may not happen and that we'll look stupid for launching things online and not getting a 'cool' response of hundreds of likes, etc. Please remember that it's going to take a little while to get to where you want but that's the beauty of aiming high, the journey will teach you so much. It takes six weeks to build a Toyota car, but it takes six months to build a Rolls Royce. You are the Rolls Royce – a model of quality, and quality takes time. If you want the world to see your worth and, metaphorically, pay for your value, then you have to take your time mastering your craft. Do not allow the things you see on social media to deter your genuine passions. Take your time and wake up every day with the intention of committing to being the best version of you. Build good habits and watch it all fall into place. But, before you aim to give yourself to others, it's important to take the time to invest in, love, build and know *yourself*.

> YOU CANNOT TRULY POUR INTO OTHERS WHEN YOU YOURSELF ARE RUNNING ON EMPTY.

An inspiring podcast

'Building You with Hayley Mulenda' is one of my favourite podcasts. Hayley is such a powerhouse and a natural born speaker. Her words will touch you, whether she's speaking at an event, on a YouTube video, Instagram Live, or on her podcast. She knows how to capture the room and speak directly to you in a space full of thousands. Her direct and unwavering nature helps to deliver her words with conviction. Every time I listen to an episode, I feel ready to go. Hayley and I share a lot of similarities in our beliefs about working hard, burnout, failure, and most of the themes in this book. We both have a no-nonsense approach to life, in that we cannot help the cards we were dealt, but we can damn well try to take control of the game from that point onwards.

Her episodes will make you question yourself in ways that you have never done before. It as though she's that friend that will always tell you the harsh truth no matter what but deliver it in the most constructive, helpful and uplifting way. In other words, this podcast takes the shape of the life coach you never knew you needed. I typically listen to her whenever I'm feeling low on energy and in need of a reminder to keep going. Hearing Hayley's energy and unwavering self-belief is something that really makes me happy and feel empowered. For so long I have seen too many young Black and brown women having their confidence sucked away by society. Whether it's through colourism, racism, a lack of support for Black businesses, being ignored by beauty brands in creating makeup to match our shades, or much more. People like Hayley help us break down some of these barriers and inspire a confident future generation of talented and multifaceted young people who are confident in what they do, and are occupying spaces that they have rightful ownership to just like their peers, without having to feel grateful for the chance or spending their days fighting imposter syndrome. Podcasts like Hayley's help me feel hopeful about achieving this in the future. I hope it will do the same for you too.

Practical steps to put yourself first before social media

Now, let's talk about the practical steps of putting yourself first and not allowing social media standards to rule you.

1. **Speak to yourself in the manner of a champion.** Zone in on your perceived weaknesses and rephrase them because they may possibly be your biggest strengths. A huge reason why other people's social media accounts can often make us feel inadequate is because we have not gone through the process of self-love. We haven't gotten comfortable with ourselves and who we are, so we are fragile enough that a stranger's picture can make us feel sad. I often hear girls from my area saying, 'Well, as a Black girl they won't take me or need me,' or 'Because I'm from a lower socioeconomic background, I lack this,' or 'I might be too inexperienced for this.' You have to snap out of this way of thinking. You must see these things as positives as this is what makes you different, and different is good. You have a perspective that many in the room don't. You can add value by bringing what you've seen to the table. Those who've used the same method for years could benefit from your fresh set of eyes. The background you come from might have made

   Zone in on your perceived weaknesses and rephrase them because they may possibly be your biggest strengths.

you innovative, independent, and someone who can work using their initiative. Having a lack of resources while growing up and STILL making it into the same room as those who did, means you are creative and know how to make the most of whatever is around you. You are a walking diamond right now, high in value and greatly needed.

2. **Grab opportunities presented to you and make the most of them!** In life, unique opportunities do not come around twice, you have to grab them with both hands and give them a try. Sometimes we might forget who we are and how qualified we are out of fear of just 'starting'. We want to wait until everything is perfect before we start, or to justify why we need to wait longer. As Nike says . . . 'Just do it!' You must vow to constantly show up for yourself. Remember you only get to live once, so you might as well do it to the best of your ability. I listened to a talk by an amazing guy a few years ago. I don't remember what the video was about or who the man was, but I do remember a key thing that he said: 'If you don't go ahead and times everything in your life by ten, no one else will.' The world will accept what you give them. Unless you show them your talents or your ideas, they will never know they existed. Show up and show out for yourself. Everything that you are manifesting today will become your future, so dream it big. Go hard or go home. Literally and figuratively. Start somewhere, anywhere, just start!

3. Set aside one hour (or more) to pour into your talents and dreams. I know it may not always be easy to start doing the things we love because of life commitments but when you can set aside at least one hour a day to pour into your talents and dreams, just do it! So, you want to be a makeup artist? Buy a mannequin and practise on it day and night during your free time. Or ask your little sister, cousin, or mum if you can borrow their face for an hour every few days so you can practise. Offer a free makeup service to friends and family to practise before launching. Apply for a three-week makeup training course at your local college that teaches beauty to students. Ask your local salon if you can shadow their in-house makeup artist. Volunteer at a video shoot as a touch-up makeup artist. Don't have a portfolio yet? Build your own! You get the gist. Don't focus on having to go from 0 to 100. You can go from 0 to 10, 10 to 30, 30 to 70, 70 to 100. Everyone has to start somewhere so go, go, go! The most important thing is to build these habits along the way to sustain them and turn them into a lifestyle.

When Life Gives You Lemons

You Lemons

HOW TO MAKE THE BEST DAMN LEMONADE
THE WORLD HAS EVER TASTED

I often sit with my mum and ask her endless questions about her life to better understand her journey. She tells me about everything she had to do for my sister and I, and I can't help but cry when I hear it. She went through so much hardship and suffering, losing the love of her life so young and being left with two young children, before having to leave them in a different country for four years. I can't imagine what that must have felt like. When my sister and I relocated to England, my mum instantly became my best friend, and we did everything together. I remember her working all the time to keep the roof over our head. She sometimes worked two jobs at once and was constantly exhausted, but we would've never known because she always kept a brave face. I was an active child and participated in lots of school clubs and I remember, no matter what, my mum would show up to everything to cheer me on. Sometimes she'd have to leave work, pop in and pop back out, or she would come home from a night shift, shower and come straight to school with no sleep. School concerts, reading competitions, plays, fashion shows, all of it, there was nothing she missed.

Growing up I always dreamed big; I believed that I could be anything I wanted to be. It was mainly when I became a teenager and was going through the university application process that things such as imposter syndrome began to kick in, but prior to this, I was as confident as could be. My mother had always raised me to believe that I could do anything and be anything that I wanted. Her unwavering confidence in me and my abilities is what has shaped my outlook on life today. My mum is the real definition of the term, 'turning lemons into lemonade'. No matter what, she always made sure we had everything we needed, maybe not in the way other children did, but in our own special and fun way. If I really wanted a Barbie doll, because she couldn't afford a new one, we woke early on a Saturday morning and walked to the local car boot sale. For those who don't know what that is, it's a junkyard where people come and sell the things they no longer want for insanely low prices. We'd go to the boot of each car hunting for a Barbie doll that cost less than £5. My mum would sift through the backs of these cars for hours until she found whatever it was that I wanted. She then explained to me that this doll would be more special than a store-bought Barbie because this one had a story to tell. This Barbie was found by us, and every scratch on her plastic body made her unique and no one else would have one like it. She did this kind of thing all the time. It made me feel so special and meant that she didn't have to break the bank and I didn't have to go without.

There were rarely times in my upbringing where I felt like I was missing out. This is a testament to my mother's parenting skills. She showed us that having few possessions didn't mean you had a meagre life. She showed us that we were rich in love and happiness. She made sure we had a wealth of morals and values and raised us to appreciate everything we had. I remember one Christmas when we received baby lotion and socks for presents. This was one of the happiest days of my childhood, and she made it exciting with a two-foot tree, and everyone wrapping up whatever they could find that the other person loved. I bought my auntie a bottle of Coke because that was her favourite drink. I decorated a rock at school with shells, paint, and various other things. I gave it to my mum as a Christmas present every year for at least three years. She loved this rock so much, and every time she received it, she would scream with joy, despite already having received it.

> HAVING SUCH A STRONG AND LOVING MOTHER RAISE ME HAS HELPED MY JOURNEY A LOT. HER UNWAVERING SUPPORT AND BELIEF IN ME AND EVERYTHING THAT I DO TAUGHT ME TO BE CONFIDENT AND APPROACH LIFE WITH A GLASS HALF-FULL ATTITUDE.

She taught me how to see the good in everything around us and make the most out of all situations, no matter how bad they were. Her values and morals played a huge role in moulding my own character and I was never afraid to try anything because I knew I would have my mother's support. Even now, at twenty-two years of age, I often ask her, 'Mum why are you so proud of me, what if I disappoint you?' and without fail she says 'Varaidzo, there is nothing you could do that I would not be proud of. I am already so proud; anything else you do now is a bonus.' She makes me feel like I am unstoppable and when I'm standing on large stages talking to hundreds of people, or filming videos that will be viewed by hundreds of thousands, her words of constant encouragement remain in my mind.

If you are a parent reading this, or perhaps want to be a parent in the future, this is something I would really recommend instilling in your children from an early age. Let them be themselves and believe in their visions – guide them of course – but allow them to also lead. Letting a child explore their passions to their maximum potential will help shape how they approach opportunities in the future and elevate their confidence levels. I loved reading as a child (as you know) and was constantly listed the fastest reader in my classes, receiving many awards for my literacy skills. My mum realised this very quickly and when I had read all the books on the shelf for my primary school class, I started reading the ones for the year above, and so on and so forth. When there was nothing else for me to read, my mother started to buy me my own books. Again, these were extremely expensive and we couldn't afford them, so the games began once more. We visited charity shops, more car boot sales and charity auctions to find the most exciting books we could. Once again, she would tell me that all the books had character and that each tea stain or missing page made the book more unique. She was truly phenomenal in showing me how to reframe situations.

LETTING A CHILD EXPLORE THEIR PASSIONS TO THEIR MAXIMUM POTENTIAL WILL SHAPE HOW THEY APPROACH OPPORTUNITIES IN THE FUTURE AND ELEVATE THEIR CONFIDENCE LEVELS.

How books helped me find peace

I used to read these books day and night. When other children were playing outside during the summer holidays, I had my head buried in a book. When the bullying at primary school began and kids began to 'see colour', books gave me an escape, something that I could look forward to, a world that felt safe and untainted. The books felt like a movie in my mind, a movie I had control of. I could press play, pause, and rewind as and when I fancied. When reading, I felt like I was in complete control, and had access to all the characters' deepest thoughts. This made me feel safe, unlike at school where I couldn't read what people were going to do next or know how they would put me down that day.

BOOKS BECAME MY FRIENDS AND REMAIN THAT WAY TODAY.

Every librarian at every school I attended knew my name as I inevitably became their most frequent visitor. I read to forget how my bullies would put their cheese and onion crisp-covered fingers into my afro during the lunch break and laugh at how they could hide in there. The questions about why my nose wasn't pointy began, and at random moments during the day someone would put their hand on their nose, press down hard and laugh at how squishy and flat it could go. Then the stereotypes kicked in and questions about my 'hut' house in Africa were rolled out and concern for my gorilla and monkey cousins were voiced. I was endlessly questioned about why I said things with an accent and ridiculed for not knowing the textual difference between read, read and red, despite English being my *second* language. I did my best to ignore these comments and hide my tears. I would tell the teachers and confide in my friends, but nothing was ever done and the following week the same incidents would occur.

The worst of the questions came on the lead-up to Father's Day. Every year we made gifts for our parents on special days like these, and every year I was made to suffer these arts and crafts days despite not having a dad. My mother had explained to the school that my father had passed away, but still, I was made to be present in the room while the other kids made gifts for their dads. Of course, as kids do, the questions about why I wasn't making something would come up. I would explain that my father was dead but the kids found it hilarious and often joked that I left him in my mud hut in Africa, or that he'd run away from me. They asked me how and why he died, a question I couldn't answer as I didn't know myself. These questions hurt me the most because of my unresolved emotions. I felt abandoned despite having the young understanding that death was unavoidable. I still felt like he had left me. To deal with my continual grief and to zone out my bullies, I found books, hence the fast reading and constant book shopping trips.

I never used to get in any sort of trouble with my mum as I never did much wrong. I was the child who always wanted to do the right thing. The only thing I remember getting in trouble for was always in relation to my obsession with books. I was often in trouble for reading a book too fast during the summer holidays. The books cost a lot of money and my mum would struggle to keep up with my fast-reading habits. If I did borrow books from the local library, I'd get through them so fast that I'd forget where I left the last one, often getting fines for not bringing them back on time, which my mum would have to pay. Another reason I got into trouble because of my books was during the night. Night-time reading before bed always has been and always will be my favourite form of reading. I loved it so much because night-time was the most peaceful and undisturbed part of my day. But my mum hated it; me reading at night meant I wouldn't sleep until that book was read. It meant I was tired in the mornings from secretly staying up to read. My mum tried everything to get me to put the books down, but I would always beg, 'One more chapter please.'

Having my books and my deep desire to learn new skills, like singing, dancing, and acting, was a form of redirecting my energy and pain. I never wanted the kids at school to see me break down. Their relentless desire to label me 'dumb', because of my accent and my background, made me so determined to prove them wrong. I used to score good grades frequently, always in the top performing group of students. With the help of my mum, I channelled my energy and the little resources we had to do good things that would support myself and those around me. I would help out in the school fundraisers, write short stories for library competitions, and do my best to make the most of my time at school and make friends. Dealing with loss, grief and pain has been something I have found difficult and a slow-burning process. As I mentioned before, my mum has always encouraged me to see life as a glass, which I should try and see as half-full rather than half-empty. She teaches me to embrace the things that are present while also having a desire to learn new skills, make new goals and more. The death of my father is something that I will learn to deal with and process as I get older. I often wonder, however, how different my life would've been if I'd had a constant male presence, someone to guide me as I navigate this complex and ever-changing world. Experiencing death at such a young age was difficult and has had a massive impact on me. But, as I go along, I am

I channelled my energy and the little resources we had to do good things that would support myself and those around me.

learning how to let people in again, addressing my fears of abandonment and accepting my past as something that has made me the strong woman that I am today. It's not easy and there are still moments when I find myself reflecting on my childhood and getting sad. Sad at what my mum had to go through, sad at what my sister and I had to go through, and sad that sometimes good people have to suffer. The sacrifices that my mum has made and continues to make for my sister and I have shaped my character and morals as an adult. Whenever I can, I try to help others to the best of my ability.

Now, would it be the end of a chapter if I didn't share a cliché that I live by? No, it would not. One of the things that I repeat to myself and to students who often feel sad about their current living or family situations is, 'You were born in the slum but the slum was not born in you.' This quote can be viewed from many different angles, but I take it to mean that we cannot choose our starting points in life but we can definitely create our own futures. Remain proud of your background and remember that your ability to adapt to difficult situations, your ability to still be standing after whatever you have gone through, shows your ability to innovate and to use the little resources that you do have around you.

PRACTICAL STEPS FOR TURNING LEMONS INTO LEMONADE

1. Find a hobby or a pastime that brings you joy and solace, that allows you to escape your current circumstances. For me, it has always been reading but for you it might be music, art, acting, etc. Reading gave me the opportunity to become one with my thoughts, to silence external noise and to focus on something else. It helped me learn how to centre myself in the midst of chaos and knowing I had the power to do something that made me feel more in control. You might find that your new hobby helps you reignite your creativity or helps you feel more relaxed, or just at one with your thoughts.

2. Find something to throw yourself into. This could be volunteering at a soup kitchen once a week, or speaking to young kids about how to tackle bullying, whatever your interests are. Sometimes it helps to take your mind off your own pain and put that energy into helping others. I found that the more I helped other people who were younger than me, the more I began to learn the skills of coping and healing. I had to give advice to those younger than me so that I could learn for myself and practise what I preached.

3. Tap into your support networks. Talking to my mum and my sister about the things that stress me out has always helped me. If you can find someone you can confide in and share your thoughts with that would be great, especially someone who is qualified and trained to deal with things like pain and emotional distress, such as a therapist or school counsellor who can encourage and support you.

Small but Powerful

HOW TO EMPOWER YOURSELF
IN WHAT YOU DO HAVE

I find that the things I have trouble speaking about are the things that confuse me the most. Some of the most hurtful things that have happened in my life often leave me questioning why they happened in the first place. One of those things happens to be the bullying that I faced while at school. It's difficult to rehash that part of my life because one part of me feels embarrassed that it happened and the other part wants to pretend it never did.

I NOW REALISE THAT HAVING THE STRENGTH TO OPENLY SHARE THE THINGS WE'VE BEEN THROUGH HELPS US TO EMPOWER OURSELVES THROUGH HEALING. IT ALSO HELPS TO EMPOWER OTHERS WHO HAVE BEEN THROUGH THE SAME THINGS.

Even if you only share what you went through with your diary, a friend or a group of people that understand, do it. I have found that the process of writing this book has helped me confront this part of my life and it's the first time I've publicly opened up about it. Sharing doesn't always have to be public, it can just be expressing your thoughts outside of your own head, i.e. in a diary.

I have spoken a bit about being bullied in primary school in the previous chapter, but the worst of the bullying came when we moved to Wales. We moved when I was about to begin my first year of high school. My mum had gotten a job there; she worked as a nurse and finding work was becoming difficult where we used to live, so when the opportunity for a higher-paying position arose, she jumped at it. At first, we loved Wales; it truly is a beautiful place, lots of greenery and a very peaceful atmosphere. We got to explore a lot of nature, take long walks and take in the fresh air; a different experience to the city-centred life we had lived in Birmingham. Something my younger self loved most about Wales was the new bedroom I now had. I loved that bedroom so much, it was just so cool and cosy. It was small, cute and had many hidden spots where I could store my books and various other prized possessions. We also attended church a lot and made many friends there who ended up feeling like a second family. Everything in Wales felt great at first, our mum was happier in her job and that radiated and translated at home, and our church social life was booming and enjoyable.

However, things took a turn for the worst when my sister and I finally began school. From the first day we arrived, Fadziee and I quickly realised we had entered a different world. There was little to no diversity of any sort. We were two of literally a handful of students who were Black in the entire school. At first, this didn't bother me, I had always been in majority white spaces so this wasn't anything new. We did however think our race would not matter so much since we were now in high school and people were more aware of why racism was bad and would generally be more accepting of one another's differences. Boy, were we wrong. It began with little comments about the size of my lips and mocking how big they were, or how I was a slightly bigger size than the other girls and PE shorts looked different on me. Then there were the typical mean moments of people laughing at the fact that I was always the last pick on the 'who would you date lists'. Any boy who dared choose me over the other girls would be mocked endlessly for a day or two. The popular girls made it clear very quickly that I literally could not 'sit' with them because 1) I was English and 2) I was Black. I would hear them laugh when I entered a classroom and move away if I tried to occupy a seat near them on the school bus or in the canteen.

It was during my stay in Wales that I stopped wearing my natural hair as an afro, the way I enjoyed it, and tried to shrink myself. Any sign of difference was pounced upon and I recall working hard to have my accent sound more like theirs and less English or Zimbabwean. I began to straighten my hair every day before school to blend in, as much as a green apple can disappear among shiny oranges. I started to demand my mum take my sister and I shopping every few months to keep up with the popular girls and their constant stream of new handbags, shoes and coats. I dreaded the times when a substitute teacher would come across my name while taking attendance. I would have to repeat my name about ten times before they got it correct and moved on. I would hear my classmates mocking my name and giggling as the teacher struggled to say it. My cheeks would burn, and I would beg for the floor to swallow me whole. I did eventually meet a group of wonderful girls, though, who welcomed me into their group and helped me get comfortable. I will never forget those girls. They could have easily followed the clear status quo and treated me the way that the others did but their kindness overrode their desire to fit in. They really gave me a lot of strength and their warmth kept me going.

I used to perform well on the tests that we were given and some of my teachers often appeared somewhat annoyed by this fact. Eventually going to school began to feel like entering a battlefield. It felt like the hostility was coming from all angles with direct racist comments and slurs from a few students were being thrown around. Even when we got home and were walking in the local area, going for a jog or shopping for food, without fail we would hear the words 'go back to your country' directed our way. My sister and I had become so distressed by the constant comments that we were becoming less confident in our identities. We begged our mum to let us move back to

England and despite her loving her job so much, she could see how unhappy we were and agreed that we should move back. In retrospect, she taught me a huge lesson while we were there. Any time I cried to her about not having enough money or not having what the popular girls had, any time I cried about wanting the constant ridiculing to end, my mum would tell me, 'If this is you without it, imagine you when you do have it.'

Once we had moved back to England I began a new high school, one that most of my friends from primary school were now attending. The school wasn't necessarily more diverse than the one in Wales, but it certainly was more welcoming and I easily felt more at home there. One thing I loved most about school was learning history. I came to love that subject so much and I'm sure it was the result of my incredible teacher, Mr Ball, and his phenomenal teaching skills. He was so great at his job because he listened carefully to his students, advised them, made class extremely fun and created a co-learning environment. Mr Ball always made sure we all felt we had ownership of our education and were allowed to shape it. He helped me feel seen again, and that my contributions were valued. His classes carried an inclusive atmosphere, something I had gone without in Wales. If there were the odd moments where a student treated me in an unkind manner, I would tell Mr Ball. He would offer me the kindest advice and tell me that the unkind people were the ones who were losing because they hadn't taken the time to know me and therefore they were the ones missing out. He really helped me realise that people's comments did not define me. He was just wonderful and I wish more students could have a teacher like him.

ONE THING I LOVED MOST ABOUT SCHOOL WAS LEARNING HISTORY. I CAME TO LOVE THAT SUBJECT SO MUCH AND I'M SURE IT WAS THE RESULT OF MY INCREDIBLE TEACHER, MR BALL, AND HIS PHENOMENAL TEACHING SKILLS. HE WAS SO GREAT AT HIS JOB BECAUSE HE LISTENED CAREFULLY TO HIS STUDENTS, ADVISED THEM, MADE CLASS EXTREMELY FUN AND CREATED A CO-LEARNING ENVIRONMENT. MR BALL ALWAYS MADE SURE WE ALL FELT WE HAD OWNERSHIP OF OUR EDUCATION AND WERE ALLOWED TO SHAPE IT. HE HELPED ME FEEL SEEN AGAIN, AND THAT MY CONTRIBUTIONS WERE VALUED.

How bullying eventually inspired me

My twelve-year-old, runny-nosed, and upset self didn't understand what my mum meant by her comment when we were still in Wales. It truly didn't register until I had become a little older. Once I understood, it became a daily mantra. Essentially, my mother's message was this: if this is you now without the things that they mock you for not having, can you imagine what you would be like when you do have everything? The answer is: unstoppable.

Whenever they laughed at my cheap school bag or the shoes that had a little hole in them, my mum would say, look at you, still shining despite not having an expensive school bag. She reminded me that I was a girl making things work without a lot of resources and that if I was lucky enough to have what they did, I could take over the world. This sentiment rings true to me today. It's something I repeat to my students when they come to me and say they're not good enough for the things they want to apply for, or for the things that they dream about because of their adversities or perceived 'lack thereof'. This especially hurts my heart because I remember feeling this way too when I was younger and wished that someone – other than my mum – had told me I was good enough and capable of doing things beyond my wildest imagination. These constant comments from the students I mentored are what truly inspired me to go ahead and start my channel, and ultimately gain an online presence. I wanted to share this story of struggle that resulted

Essentially, my mother's message was this: if this is you now without the things that they mock you for not having, can you imagine what you would be like when you do have everything? The answer is: unstoppable.

in triumph. I wanted students from backgrounds like mine to
see themselves represented in spaces that have been socially
closed off to us. I wanted to put myself out there and show
off everything I had become since primary school when I was
mocked for my afro hair or crying my eyes out in Wales because
I desperately wanted to fit in.

I WANTED THE YOUNG GIRLS I CAME ACROSS
TO FEEL EMPOWERED IN WHO THEY WERE,
SOMETHING I WANTED TO FEEL WHEN I WAS
YOUNGER. I WANTED THEM TO GO THROUGH LIFE
WITH THEIR HEADS HELD HIGH, AND WITH THE
SKILLS AND TOOLS THEY NEEDED TO THRIVE
AND SURVIVE.

The channel began out of the sheer determination to show the
doubters, bullies, and dismissive teachers what happens when
you combine academic talent with perseverance. I wanted
them to see us, the community of young people defying the
odds that were set against them. I wanted to show others
who looked or sounded like me that the sky was the limit and
provide the helpful resources and tools that would help them
get to where they wanted to be. I shouted about opportunities
such as the Social Mobility Foundation, the charity programme
I was a part of at the age of sixteen. They helped relieve the
biggest barrier and stress in my life: finances. My mum couldn't
afford to have me go around the UK viewing every university I
was interested in but I was determined to do so because I knew
it was a vital part of my future and the decision I was about

to make. The Social Mobility Foundation paid for everything, from travel to food and sometimes, if students needed it, accommodation so that we could go and visit the universities that we hoped to apply for. They offered personal statement guidance, mock interviews and Q&A sessions with previous SMF members who had gone on to university. Opportunities like these exist and many students don't know about it. I, for one, know that the SMF changed my life and helped open doors I wouldn't have been able to access otherwise. The SMF can also be given credit for unlocking my inner go-getter, mostly because they provided me access to speaker events where I could meet students in the worlds of banking, law and finance, but also those who had attended Oxford, Cambridge, Warwick, and various other Russell Group schools.

When I was seventeen I needed work experience and an internship so that my CV would look impressive for the universities I wanted to apply for. I received an email from the SMF about a summer residential internship at JP Morgan in London. I had never lived in London before but had always wanted to go, and a banking internship at a place like JP Morgan was insane, so I applied. I can't begin to express the scream I let out when they told me I'd been selected to attend the internship for two weeks of the summer, all expenses paid. My time on that internship showed me that I had the potential to be so much more. It was the first time I had sat with managing directors. They took us out to lunch and gave advice and shared the stories of their humble beginnings. This internship, although I had no interest in banking, opened my eyes. It exposed me to something different, which I wasn't getting at home. I came back that summer feeling revolutionised. I was shown that there was a different way of life to what I had seen at home or at my part-time job at McDonalds.

I WANTED TO SHOW OTHERS WHO LOOKED OR SOUNDED LIKE ME THAT THE SKY WAS THE LIMIT AND PROVIDE THE HELPFUL RESOURCES AND TOOLS THAT WOULD HELP THEM GET TO WHERE THEY WANTED TO BE.

I returned to JP Morgan a few more times for other spring weeks and mini-internships and every time I went back, I grew in strength, knowledge, and confidence. I had had a taste of what a life of financial freedom and independence was like and I wanted it. The SMF kept in contact with us throughout, sharing various career opportunities that came up and showing us a wealth of options that I didn't even know existed. At my local school we had been told we could become teachers, nurses, or social workers, and that's where the list truly ended. That was all we saw around us. Programmes like the SMF give students from lower socioeconomic backgrounds a chance to see beyond their immediate community. There are, of course, other programmes similar to this all over the UK and such as Digital Futures, Rare Recruitment, Future Leaders, Target Oxbridge, Amos Bursary, The Brilliant Club, The Grant Fairy and more. The SMF however, is the specific organisation that I personally relied on from ages sixteen to eighteen and it really helped me. Therefore, when it came time to create my channel, I knew it needed to include crucial opportunities like this to help other students fulfil their dreams *despite* them not having the financial ability to do so.

I remember filming my first video and being afraid that no one would watch it and that people would laugh at me. I worried that maybe I needed to wait until I had the microphones, the right lighting, the right clothes, etc. I once again approached my fountain of wisdom, my mother, and asked her for advice and – yep, you guessed it – she repeated her wise old saying. 'If this is what you can do now without all the fancy stuff, imagine what you can do a year from now. Just start.' She told me that it didn't matter if people laughed at me. So long as someone, even just one person, gained something useful from the content, then it outweighed the potential negative comments. I remember her sitting on the sofa while I recorded one of my first videos, just cheering me on and making the cheesiest smiles. My nerves instantly went away and two years later here we are writing a book, with over 250,000 subscribers and a global community.

> STARTING THAT CHANNEL WAS THE BEST THING I'VE EVER DONE AND HAS CHANGED THE SHAPE OF MY LIFE FOREVER. I'VE BEEN ABLE TO CONNECT WITH SO MANY STUDENTS AND YOUNG PEOPLE ON A PERSONAL LEVEL WHILE SHOWCASING THE REALITIES FOR MANY STUDENTS WITH STORIES LIKE MINE.

Starting my YouTube channel has allowed me to become a part of something bigger than my own journey. I get to build a community with like-minded young people, lean on them for advice, and use them as my source of inspiration and reason to wake up every day and do better. I get to make an impact on people living in difficult situations and in need of uplifting and empowering. I help them find their voices again and turn their lemons into lemonade through mentoring and exposure to a wealth of opportunities created just for them. Taking that leap of faith to do something about a problem that I kept seeing around me has turned into something bigger than I could have ever imagined. On my channel, I would regularly post videos about my experiences applying for university, share study tips and showcase the reality of being a minority at an elite and privileged university surrounded by people with outstanding amounts of money. Every time I shared myself online, I read comments about the impact that the content was having on people, how it was changing their mindsets and encouraging them to do things they never thought would be possible just because they finally believed in themselves. Seeing me being unapologetic about where I came from, and my entrance into Oxford through an unconventional route inspired them. At first, I was shocked by this. I thought the sole reason viewers watched my channel was to gather information about the various organisations and opportunities I had to share. I didn't think a video of me simply living a day in my life could do so much for young Black girls across the globe. Everything that's happened in my life since would have never happened if I'd allowed my fears to take over. I had to take that leap of faith to follow my heart and allow my desire to help lead me.

You can't view trying to make an impact or a change as something that will happen only when you're a superstar with millions of followers.

My best friend Malala, an incredible soul with the most genuine of hearts, always tells me that it's not about starting big but just starting. She calls it the small but mighty approach and I call it the small but powerful outlook: two sides of the same coin. Essentially, you can't view trying to make an impact or a change as something that will happen only when you're a superstar with millions of followers. It can happen now, today in your community, and with the people you care for and want to serve. To make an impact, the world doesn't have to know your name, it doesn't have to be something that touches thousands of people, it can be something that causes generational change for ten families or for a specific group of people. Share your story. You never know who it could help and what difference you can make in people's lives. You also don't have to invent a problem that doesn't exist or be the next person to discover gravity for what you do to mean something. Just look around and find what it is that makes you want to help.

A great example of small but powerful is the platform that I've had the honour of building called 'Empowered by Vee'. It began because students wanted to have a coffee with me, and I was finding it difficult to try and meet everyone while also maintaining my university life. I organised a day in which students would come down to my campus. I arranged for speakers who were just like them to come in and share their experiences, offer practical advice, and help empower the students. The first time I planned the event, we had just under 100 students come along and join us. The event was a great success and I was extremely happy. For months after, I was getting messages from students about how much it had helped them and how they were using the advice they'd received to shape their lives. I believed that was as big as the event was going to get and never in a million years did I think we'd have a community of nearly 5,000 students benefiting from the platform. So, whether it's 5 . . . 500 . . . 5,000 . . . or five million people that you're impacting, you're still making a huge difference.

Here's another cliché that I love: 'Build it and they will come.' Create that initiative you're thinking about and those who need it will find you. Better yet, take your skills and story to an organisation already working for what you're passionate about. People often forget that there's great power in helping build on what already exists. There are many phenomenal organisations tackling the very things you care about who need extra volunteers. This is the perfect opportunity to take your story, your pain, and transform it into something good that can help others. In the process, you're also helping you. Looking back at the things I went through in my journey of self-discovery, I wish I could've learned those lessons without having to experience all the sadness. Nevertheless, I'm glad that I did because it's shaped me into the resilient, emotionally aware and giving person that I am today. Taking my pain and turning it into a purpose is something I don't regret doing and would do again. If you're experiencing hardship right now, I promise you better days are ahead.

Practical steps towards starting small

1. **Be proactive.** Seeing those around me doing well and thriving despite the odds brings me great joy. The world is our oyster and with the right tools, support, and access to opportunities we can do the things we truly desire. If you're in need, reach out to groups around you, and ask your schools or universities to point you to the right places. There are many organisations that help young people from underrepresented, unsupported, and underfunded backgrounds. They provide you with bursaries and scholarships that you don't have to pay back. They also have partnerships with various firms and universities and can help you gain access to opportunities like internships, jobs and more. As mentioned, the SMF is just one of those organisations, but there are many others out there, it's just a matter of finding them by searching on Google, typing in keywords on LinkedIn and Instagram such as 'access', 'bridging the gap', 'supporting students', 'supporting black students', 'addressing underrepresentation', or 'tackling underrepresentation at top universities'.

2. **If you can, report it.** If you're currently facing bullying and have no one to speak to or are starting to believe what the bullies say, remember that you are *not* deserving of how you are being treated. You must make sure you report what is happening to you and if they aren't doing anything about it, consider sharing with your legal guardian or HR if there is bullying in the workplace. We can't let these people win because they'll start to believe that they are right. Fight bad with good. You can prove these people wrong by simply proving yourself right. More often than not when people mistreat others, it's because they are projecting, they are feeling insecure, or perhaps have been bullied themselves. Go ahead and continue focusing on yourself, shining brighter than any star and using your talents to live *your* life.

3. **Pay it forward.** If you are a person who has already made their dreams come true and had a similar rocky start to life, consider ways that you could help the next generation on their journey, if you can. Young people are the future, and to invest in them is to invest in the world. There are many ways to get involved, either by running your own organisation, helping one that already exists by volunteering or simply donating money to them, so they can continue doing the work to support young people.

Money, Money, Money

HOW TO FEEL FINANCIALLY EMPOWERED (NO MATTER WHAT YOUR BANK ACCOUNT LOOKS LIKE)

I'm no expert when it comes to money, but I've learned a thing or two along the way about what it can do for you and what life feels like without it. As you know, I was born and raised in Zimbabwe before moving to England at the age of six. I didn't consider money a lot when I was in Zimbabwe because I was a child and didn't understand its true value. I just knew that I wished for more toys and better food, but I didn't equate this to a lack of money. When I came to England, the same thing carried over. My mother, as previously mentioned, was fantastic at making something out of nothing. No matter how rock bottom we were, she made it work. She would shop at the discounted, about-to-expire sections of supermarkets, always bought the supermarket value items, and a lot of the time we visited food banks. To us, it all felt normal. I didn't know any different and found it fun to hunt out the bargains. It's only with hindsight and growing older that I can see the various ways of life we adapted to because my mum couldn't afford the 'standard'.

Money played a huge role in what we wore, ate, and had access to. Our school uniforms were always purchased two sizes up, so that there was room to grow into them. Day-to-day clothing came from charity shops or was handed down from church cousins, unless of course it was my birthday, then an outfit from a store was permitted. I recall losing my 'to grow into' pair of trousers after an adventure school trip where we had changed into PE kits. The next day I had to wear my old trousers, ones that were far too small and visibly no longer my size. It was at the end of the school day when parents were picking up their children that we heard one of the parents laugh and point at me, saying she didn't understand why my mum never just bought us the right sized clothes. I know she won't admit it, but I know this hurt my mother's feelings. I noticed that after a few weeks she was more tired than usual (from working longer hours to make extra money) but she took us shopping, got us a new school wardrobe and from that day forth, we wore the right size uniform.

Money makes a difference. As we got older, I noticed that my mum became happier; the more experienced she became at work, the more she began to earn. She loved her job as a nurse and worked extremely hard. We were now trying new food, shopping outside of charity shops and I was getting brand new books. It was delightful to see her gain a new sense of independence and feel like she was providing enough for us. I always say that even when she had little to no money, my mum always provided for us, but for her, she felt more validated when she could financially do more for us. She used to tell me how she hated the feeling of seeing other children have exactly what their hearts desired while my sister and I always had to have the alternative versions of everything. As soon as I was old enough to understand, she began to teach my sister and I lessons on how to be responsible with money so that we would never have to go through the things that she did.

She began by opening children's bank accounts for us and she would show us how to withdraw money from there. She would give us £10 each a week for our dinners at high school. She never gave us more than £10, in order to teach us how to budget and how to spend wisely. On average, a standard school meal was £2 and with five days in a week £10 was the exact amount. However, the temptation of random snacks, extras, etc., meant that £2 a day could easily be misused and for the first few weeks, I struggled with staying within budget. Eventually, however, I learned. This responsibility early on taught me how to think ahead and not just within the moment. Yes, I would've enjoyed that £5 meal on Monday, but it meant I'd be crying on Friday. We went on this way with our £10 a week and my sister and I were happy; we wished we had a little more, but we were happy. We had friends whose parents gave them £15 to £20 a week and they almost always had nothing left by the time Friday would arrive. I think because they had so much, they didn't value it and spent their allowance on snacks, gum, and drinks without much consideration. At first, I didn't understand it. I truly thought that having more money at your disposal meant that it'd be easier to manage and was surprised to see these kids complaining it had run out before the school week was over. I now understand the lesson my mum taught me and have carried it over into my adult life. We eventually got upgraded to £15 a week but by that point my sister and I were so used to having £10 that we saved the extra £5 for things we didn't want to ask our mum to get such as makeup, jewellery, and other little bits and bobs. We became financially aware at a young age and understood the power of the pound.

My mum also used to task my sister and I with managing what we wanted to eat at home and things of this nature. She would ask us to help write out the food shopping list and when we went to the shops, we were in charge of making sure we were on budget. This taught us the value of money and what it can and cannot buy. It also taught us not to be wasteful because we knew the cost of things. Once again, with every lesson, our mum made it all fun and enjoyable. She taught us to have a healthy relationship with money and to see it as something transactional that can give you access to goods, and those goods were the things that made you happy – not necessarily the money itself.

> (Mum) taught us to have a healthy relationship with money and to see it as something transactional that can give you access to goods, and those goods were the things that made you happy – not necessarily the money itself.

When I turned sixteen, I got my first job. I was eager to make my own money. I wanted independence but I also wanted to support my mum's smaller financial burdens such as my phone bill, dinner money, money for clothes, books, etc. I began making £4.16 an hour while working part-time, alongside studying. This experience taught me how to become extremely responsible at a young age, ensuring I worked enough to support my leisure time but also that I still made time to study for school and maintain my grades. I worked at McDonalds for a year and in the process saved money to fund my summer activities, such as flying to America for three months to take part in Camp America. I was good at saving and knew the value of a budget. It helped me grow a healthy relationship with money and not see it as a source of temptation as many of my friends did.

After my time at McDonalds, I maintained a few other part-time retail jobs while finishing my A-Levels and only stopped working once I got a place at Oxford University. At Oxford, we were told we could not have part-time jobs because of the intensity of our studies. Bursaries, scholarships, and other helpful pots of funding supplemented the money we would've made. Stepping into this world was a strange feeling. Going from working and providing for myself while studying for A-Levels to being told I couldn't work was a hard transition. I felt guilty to just be given money that I didn't feel I had earned. I had assumed all my friends would feel the same way but came to discover that working while studying was not the norm for many of my university peers. This is when I realised that just because we were all eighteen-year-old freshers at university, it didn't mean we had all experienced the same 'hardships'. Back home, in Birmingham, working while studying was the norm as we all knew we had no other choice, however for many of my friends at Oxford, money was never an issue, there was no urgency or desire for them to work prior to university. Of course, the ideal would be that all students feel they have a choice about whether they want to work as opposed to feeling they have to in order to survive. I was just shocked that two young people could have such drastically different experiences of the same periods in their life. I came to learn that sixth-form colleges (a place of study for sixteen-to-eighteen-year-olds here in the UK) could cost more than university itself. A lot of my peers at Oxford explained that their schooling had cost their parents between £15,000 and £25,000 a year. I remember my jaw genuinely dropping when I first heard this. I hadn't realised just how huge the disparity could be.

I had to quickly adjust to the new space that I was in, going from earning £4.16 an hour and budgeting £160 per month, to now hearing that one Fancy Ball or Gala ticket could cost £200, a dress would be another £150, and return transport would be an additional £50. My heart fell out of my chest. I had never spent this kind of money before, nor had anyone in my family. Even with my bursary and student finances, after the rent was paid, along with the costs of my core textbooks, food shopping, and various other bits, there wasn't much left. I wasn't in the same position as my friends who could call home and ask for top-ups. If anything, I was sometimes sending money to my family to help them make ends meet, so I had no choice but to stay within my budget.

I FELT COMPLETELY OUT OF PLACE AND WAS ONCE AGAIN REMINDED OF WHAT HAVING MONEY CAN DO FOR YOU AND WHAT NOT HAVING IT FELT LIKE.

I saw some of my friends receive thousands, and I genuinely mean thousands of pounds per month from their parents to supplement their spending habits. Once again, similar to my friends at high school, their money never lasted, it was always gone before the end of the month and I came to the realisation that it's not necessarily about how much you have, rather it's about how you spend it. If you don't have money management skills, it doesn't get better by simply having more money to manage. As the saying goes, if you can't manage £100, then you can't manage £1,000.

How I developed a revenue stream online

During my time at Oxford, I started a YouTube channel to showcase my experience there and how I was settling in and navigating the space as a young Black woman from a lower socioeconomic background. YouTube for me was a creative outlet, a space that I used to express myself and encourage others who may have felt unsupported while at university or with their upcoming applications. Never in a million years did I consider that I could make money on the platform. I didn't earn anything until around one year of uploading content online. My first pay cheque was £113. I was financially struggling at university this particular month. I just remember feeling so happy to receive that paycheque that I cried – I didn't expect my videos to ever make any money so the £113 came as a surprise. I now had a consistent source of income in larger sums than I had ever had before. My channel began to pick up more and more and soon £113 a month became £300 a month. Over time, I had a steady £200 to £300 coming into my account monthly. This helped me sustain myself, on top of the student finance from the university. When I received my first four-figure cheque from YouTube I had to blink hard. I was astonished that I was now able to make a living monthly wage from doing what I loved. I was so used to seeing the balance in my bank account in the hundreds that I thought they'd made a mistake that month. I didn't touch the money for a few weeks just in case. After that, it became standard that my videos would make between £700 and £1,000 a month. I couldn't believe how quickly things had changed financially for me.

In the same breath that my videos began making more, I got signed to a management agency. Having management meant that I no longer had to do my own negotiations with the brands, it meant I was now advised on how to grow my platforms and create content that was of a high quality. It relieved me of the stresses of the admin side of things and gave me more time to study and create videos that I loved.

Getting management is still one of the craziest things that has happened in my life generally, but especially financially. With YouTube, you are paid via adverts and according to how many people watch your videos, for how long, and so on. It works in a similar way to other creative platforms like Medium, SkillShare or Fiver. With YouTube, as well as the watchtime payments, you will also have brands approach you to advertise their items in your videos for a fee. Prior to having management, I would charge between £80 and £400 depending on the style of video, the brand, etc., and I would have one or two brand deals every other month. My management team was now negotiating with the brands on my behalf and managing to get deals that were almost ten times higher than what I was making alone. They would source the deals, negotiate them and then help me with keeping my content on track and true to what I stood for. This is the point when YouTube became my full-time job, something I had never dreamed of happening. The same brand that paid me £300 for a full ten-to-twelve-minute video was now paying me over £3,000 or more for the same thing. I couldn't believe my eyes. I couldn't believe the financial side of this industry was not spoken about. I tried to look for people discussing their pay online and could not find it. The reason why I did not have the ability to negotiate higher fees for myself without management was that I did not know the industry well. My management, on the other hand, knew just how big the brands' budgets were, so they were able to negotiate higher fees on my behalf. Thus the pattern took shape: the more I grew online as a content creator, the more money I was able to make.

Now, I will admit, for a girl who came from my background, having more than £800 in my bank account was extremely scary. At first, I didn't know what to do with it. Of course, my instinct to provide kicked in and a large chunk of the money was spent on my family and friends. I remember reaching 100,000 subscribers on YouTube and getting paid an insane amount that month too. I immediately decided I wanted to throw a party for my family and friends to thank them for supporting me on this journey and helping me get to where I was. At the same time, I had this huge sense of guilt that loomed over me constantly. I had watched those around me work tirelessly in the most meaningful professions, like nursing, and knew that I was making in a month what they would take several months to even save. I felt a responsibility to share what I was making as I didn't believe it fair for me to earn that just from sharing myself on the internet. It was the same guilt I felt from getting into and attending Oxford, when I knew there were people at home who were way smarter than me and who wanted to be there but were robbed of the chance just because of the area we came from.

At first, I didn't use the lessons of saving and money management that my mum had taught me. I felt so scared that the paycheques would eventually stop, so I figured, while I have it, I'm going to make sure my friends, family and I enjoy it. There was almost an imposter syndrome that came with the money. I felt as though I didn't deserve it or that at some point, these brands would soon take it away because they might feel the same way. These thoughts were on my mind constantly and it's not until I got an accountant that I stopped. We quickly figured out that the imposter syndrome I was experiencing about the money made me feel so detached from it that I wanted to spend it unwisely. Once we sat down and they helped me realise I had rightfully earned it, they also helped me to see that it was a steady source of income and that I needed to start treating it accordingly. That's when I went back to my mum's lessons and tricks, the systems I had implemented when I worked at McDonalds and while at university. I now have my healthy relationship with money back, but I think it's important that I share that imposter syndrome experience with you because it's something I have witnessed among young people from backgrounds like mine. There's this sense of disbelief, guilt or unfamiliarity when we enter well-paid roles. I have many people message me online about this, how they leave work feeling guilty at seeing those around them work extremely hard without being financially rewarded.

WHAT I WANT TO SAY IS, THE SAME WAY THAT YOU HAVE TO WORK AT FEELING EMPOWERED IN YOUR EMOTIONS, IN SEEING REJECTION AS REDIRECTION, IN EVERYTHING ELSE THAT YOU DO, YOU MUST IMPLEMENT THE SAME PRACTICE WITH FINANCES.

Someone who puts this perfectly is the legendary Hayley Mulenda. Apart from her earlier advice about comparing your life to another person's Instagram highlights, she also talks openly on her podcast, 'Building You with Hayley Mulenda', about how society sees money as the F word. A word that should not be discussed, disclosed, or thought about. But the truth of the matter is, as she so perfectly puts it, we need money to make the world go around. It's the currency we trade with, which people who have the goods value. Whether we like it or not, we have to get comfortable with having conversations about money. We have to have honest conversations about how we make our money, how we manage it, and how to have a healthy relationship with it.

NO MATTER HOW
MUCH OF IT YOU
HAVE, YOU NEED TO
HAVE A HEALTHY
RELATIONSHIP
WITH MONEY, IN
PREPARATION FOR
WHEN YOU DO
HAVE A LOT OF IT.

Women and self-confidence

Something else that I've noticed, from assessing the messages that I receive, is that imposter syndrome, when it comes to money, tends to be experienced by more women than men. Women, you have to understand that confidence is everything and we cannot allow those constant whispers of self-doubt in our minds to win, because there are men, many men, who are less qualified than you who are making more and don't bat an eyelid or second guess themselves. My favourite author Chimamanda Ngozi-Adichie puts it perfectly: '*We teach girls to shrink themselves, to make themselves smaller. We say to girls, "You can have ambition, but not too much, you should aim to be successful, but not too successful, otherwise you will threaten the man,"'* and I couldn't agree more.

As young women, especially young women from Black or ethnic minority groups, we're made to feel as though we should constantly be grateful for everything we get, to aim high but not too high so as not to make others around us feel uncomfortable. I remember sitting among some of my male peers, having a conversation about trading and finances, and I was made to feel as if I couldn't contribute. They were bragging to each other about how much they had and how much their investments had gained in the last year. In that moment I could've opened my mouth to add to the conversation but felt as though I shouldn't in case I wasn't believed. The point here is that they were talking to each other and I was not included in the conversation because they believed I had nothing to add. Or, maybe that I *shouldn't* have anything to add. This notion of speaking without including us in the conversation is common, with men typically making decisions about finances and then allowing women into the conversation as and when they feel they should be included. If finances were discussed openly, the gender pay gap could be better addressed. We'd then have insight into what others doing the *same* job as us were making regardless of their gender.

THIS IS YOUR LIFE AND YOU MUST LIVE IT. USE YOUR MONEY WISELY, OWN IT AND STOP APOLOGISING FOR WINNING.

I can now comfortably admit that for a young person, I'm making a lot of money and that's okay. I try to no longer feel guilt and instead use my money wisely to live my life but also help others where I can. I make sure I contribute to charities that are supporting young people from underrepresented backgrounds with access to education. I do this because there were times when I felt financially burdened and wished I could focus on my studies instead of money. As long as you're giving back where you can and using your money responsibly, you must learn to embrace it.

The first step to having a healthy relationship with money is seeing it as something that gives you access.

The first step to having a healthy relationship with money is seeing it as something that gives you access. It doesn't make you better than anyone else, it doesn't mean you can treat others in a disrespectful manner or make others feel less than because they don't earn the same. Money isn't a reflection of someone's character, their morals or values. It's simply something that gives us access to things, i.e. goods, properties, luxuries, food, and clothes. It gives us financial stability, alleviates stress and allows us to do things that can make our lives easier.

Practical steps to feeling empowered in your finances

Once you've found the strength to empower yourself in your abilities, how do you get comfortable with making money and erasing the imposter syndrome about how much you make?

1. **Build a healthy relationship with money by budgeting.** It's important to learn how to budget the money that you do have and to live within your means. I have seen so many people going broke trying to act rich. When you begin to live a lifestyle that is not yours, you will end up worse off than you began. You will feel the pressure to maintain your lifestyle and you will struggle. When I worked at McDonalds and had to help my mum here and there, plus sustain myself and my phone bill, I made sure I budgeted and lived according to my pay and my responsibilities. I would walk almost everywhere and would avoid eating out at all costs (apart from the £1.99 meal deals at Chicken Hut with the girls – those were an exception). There were also more simple things that I would do that helped me budget effectively, such as using meal deal voucher codes that you can find in newspapers or magazines; shopping for clothes in the sales sections; always asking for student discounts and what offers are available before you make a purchase. These little steps can help you still enjoy the things you love, but in a way that is within your budget and lifestyle.

2. **Find a side hustle.** There is always one way or another to make extra cash while you are trying to build and save for your dreams. I remember working weekends at my uncle's restaurant. My responsibilities consisted of

manning the till, taking out the trash and cleaning the toilets. I really hated that job but loved what it taught me. I would look forward to payday because I knew I had really earned every single penny and that it was mine. I also remember playing music at the local under-eighteens club and making about £3 per ticket that my friends and I sold. This was great fun and it allowed me to use my talent to raise some extra cash. So, wherever you can, try and find a side hustle that will allow you to have an extra source of revenue. This doesn't have to be anything big because you do not want to burn yourself out or overwhelm yourself. Find something that you can do on the side, something small to start out so you can still focus on your other priorities. For example, my priority was university but on the side I was making videos once a week, which did not interfere with my university work or tire me out too much.

3. Listen to money podcasts and read some books. As I mentioned earlier, Hayley touches upon money in her podcast *Building You with Hayley Mulenda*, but you can still search for other podcasts dealing with the subject of money. I also recommend checking out books about why people may be uncomfortable with money or with talking about it. One that I would recommend is *How to Save It: Fix Your Finances* by Bola Sol, which is a short book that talks about the effective and practical ways of saving money. She discusses how a little money stashed to the side but on a regular basis can go a long way.

MONEY ISN'T INHERENTLY BAD.
IT'S WHAT WE CHOOSE TO DO
WITH IT THAT GIVES IT MEANING.
SO, IF YOU HAVE ACCESS
TO LARGER SUMS OF MONEY
DON'T FEEL GUILTY, DON'T FEEL
IMPOSTER SYNDROME, JUST
MAKE SURE WHAT YOU DO WITH
THE MONEY IS IN LINE WITH
YOUR VALUES, YOUR MORALS,
AND THAT ULTIMATELY YOU
BUILD A HEALTHY RELATIONSHIP
WITH YOUR FINANCES.

My journey, although hard, has also had a large amount of luck play into it. I accidentally found YouTube and within a year it went on to change my life and my financial situation forever. This might not be the case for someone who's been on YouTube for ten years or more. I don't think it'd be fair to simply say follow your hobbies and passions and the money will follow because sometimes it doesn't. What I can say is that once you start making money through whatever means you have access to, try to embrace it and work on creating a positive and healthy relationship with it. In the wise words of Hayley, *'Money is innocent, money is neutral ground . . . think of a knife, you can use it to cut up food, to cook, to feed and to nourish your soul and body. So that means a knife can contribute to good, but a knife can also contribute to bad. You can also do serious harm to someone through things like knife crime and stabbings. But we can't say that that was down to knives because the power was not in the knife, the power was in the hands of the person who used it.'* The way she summarises the nature of money in her podcast is so helpful. It demonstrates the power we have over how we choose to use our money and that if we want it to do good, we should simply use it for good. Money isn't inherently bad. It's what we choose to do with it that gives it meaning. So, if you have access to larger sums of money don't feel guilty, don't feel imposter syndrome, just make sure what you do with the money is in line with your values, your morals, and that ultimately you build a healthy relationship with your finances.

Building Healthy Relationships

HOW TO EMPOWER YOUR FRIENDSHIPS, PARTNERSHIPS AND 'FAMILY-SHIPS'

When things began to pick up for me online my mum often asked me how I managed to decipher who was real, who was not, and who had an ulterior motive versus who was genuine. To this day, I can openly say, I don't know. Only time can ever tell. All I can do is give the people around me the benefit of the doubt and allow their actions to speak for them. I am 90 per cent confident in my abilities to read people, and believe those nearest and dearest to me are genuine and have my best interests at heart. The 10 per cent of the time that I do get it wrong hurts, but I'm slowly learning to unlearn this, and understand that you only know what you know. You can't be to blame for not knowing someone's true intentions and sometimes you just can't see it coming. It took me a little while to get my head around this and come to the realisation that all I can control in this life are my actions and how I react to those of others. Before I discovered this, however, I used to blame myself for not seeing the betrayal coming, whether in romantic relationships, friendships, or family-ships. I often thought, 'Damn Vee, you should've known better.'

As time goes on, I'm also learning the art of forgiveness and giving people a second chance. I won't advise you to do the same because all situations are different. It truly depends on the extent of the betrayal, but I believe when someone has made a genuine mistake and they didn't intend to hurt us, we should open our hearts to hearing them out. Unless, of course, whatever they have done is simply not something you can forgive, let alone forget. Those things are deserving of terminating relationships, but smaller events can be worked through.

I remember having a difficult conversation with my childhood best friend, Kim, when we decided to call it quits on our fourteen-year friendship. We had had a stable relationship for at least eleven of those fourteen years, always side by side and generally understanding of each other. The friendship was almost like a marriage. We did everything together. Her parents allowed her to be at our house for the majority of the week (she lived a six-minute walk away from me). We were like sisters and my mum treated Kim like her own child. We used to be incredibly close and it was difficult for anyone outside of our bubble to infiltrate that. Kim was the one who helped me learn English when I first arrived in England. Even when I moved to Wales, her parents drove her across the country so she could come and visit, and when they couldn't bring her, we wrote each other letters. Receiving Kim's letters in the mail was one of the highlights of my week and somehow the distance made us closer. When I moved back to England, I enrolled in her high school and we once again became inseparable. We rarely had fights and when we did, it was over small things that we would laugh about later.

Everything was wonderful up until the point of going to university. I went away to Oxford and Kim was finishing up her final year of college before heading off to another university the following year. This meant I was the one physically leaving, and she was the one physically staying. We promised to stay close. She promised to visit all the time. We bought each other matching friendship necklaces and said our goodbyes. It's safe to say that both of us drastically underestimated the nature of university and the distance it would instantly create. Kim was still at home, in the same environment, with the same people and missing her best friend while I was in my Fresher's Week, living away from home, with new friends, new freedom, and an eagerness to explore the city. I was instantly sucked into the Oxford bubble of studying 24/7, hanging out at formal dinners, and trying to join every society on earth while also doing voluntary work. My schedule became insanely busy and the enjoyment of the new city made me forget about home.

Where I would've spoken to my best friend four or five times a week on the phone, or even every day, I was now just sending a quick text on the weekend or having a ten-minute call before having to run off to the next activity. This naturally created a distance between us. Kim didn't know much about my new life and felt as though I was intentionally dismissing her and staying in my Oxford bubble. This, of course, was not the case from my side. I was simply a new university student trying to savour the experience without missing home too much.

The thing is, we both felt the distance and didn't know how to deal with it but never said anything. She would see updates about my new life online without me telling her and feel as though I was purposefully shutting her out. I noticed that she wasn't engaging with my updates, and assumed she didn't want to know, so I never bothered filling her in. When summer holidays came around, instead of going home, I was travelling. I wanted to see the world and Oxford encouraged us to be culturally aware, often funding part of our trips through more bursaries and scholarships. I was now spending around two months of the year at home, and this was spread throughout the year. When I was home for a few days, I'd see my family, sleep, repack my bags, and maybe squeeze in a catch-up with my best friend before jetting back to university or travelling. The cycle continued for the duration of my time at university. We simply never addressed the elephant in the room and before we knew it, three years had passed and by then we'd reached a point of ultimate toxicity. We were no longer communicating effectively. We were sometimes angry with each other without being able to express why, instead snapping at one another.

An incident occurred at her birthday party where I felt truly disrespected, and finally it was time to talk. We sat at McDonald's, as you do, and had the difficult conversation we'd been avoiding, finally sharing the frustrations which had built up over the past few years. We mutually decided that things were no longer the same. I voiced that we had truly not been best friends for the last three years but were using the title out of respect for the length of our friendship. I made the difficult decision to walk away from the person I'd known for almost 70 per cent of my life and who had been by my side since I arrived in England. We had ultimately broken up as best friends. I always tell people that this was by far the hardest breakup I've ever experienced. I genuinely lost someone who meant the world to me, who I trusted with my deepest secrets, who could read me like a book. We had experienced many firsts together, cried together, and practically been raised together. Leaving this friendship broke my heart and I cried about it for a while, but I knew it was the right thing to do because had we continued as we were, we would've hated each other. It had gotten to a point where I'd purposefully hide my good news from her because I feared she would be upset by it or it would cause a 'why did you not tell me this was happening' argument. That's not how any friendship or relationship is supposed to be. Despite the hurt I was feeling about it ending, I knew that in order to preserve our mental health, sanity and peace, it was the right thing to do.

During our separation, I felt like I found myself again, and so did Kim. We were able to experience things alone, discover our own interests, explore who we were as individuals and how to stand on our own two feet. We formed new friendships, gained new experiences, and lived our lives. It was not until a year had gone by that we initiated contact with one another once again. We took things slowly, leaving the odd comment on each other's social media accounts, before having full conversations via text. We eventually decided to meet up and talk. I still stand by this today, that conversation was one of the best we've ever had. We were finally communicating, *really* communicating, and hearing each other out. Kim apologised for how she had been with me, keeping me at arms' length, and not being supportive. She explained how the frustrations stemmed from other things going on in her life and because I was the closest to her, she may have taken it out on me. During the time away from each other, she addressed the deep-rooted issues and felt more at peace with the situation. I could see it in her. It was written all over her face, she was genuinely happy. I apologised for not having realised the extent of her unhappiness and felt guilty for not having been there. I apologised for shutting down and not letting her in. I'd created a barrier between my 'at-home' life and my new life at Oxford, abroad and online. We went back and forth and addressed the things we were sorry for and by the end of the conversation we were laughing. Just like old times.

IN RETROSPECT, WE'D NOT ALLOWED OURSELVES TO BE ADULT VERSIONS OF 'US' IN OUR FRIENDSHIP. WE WERE BOUND TO THE 'RULES' WE HAD CREATED WHEN WE WERE SEVEN YEARS OLD AND HAD NOT ADVANCED BEYOND THAT FOR YEARS. WHEN NEW ELEMENTS WERE INTRODUCED AND OUR ADULT LIVES BEGAN TO FORM, WE DIDN'T KNOW HOW TO ADJUST AND THE BARRIERS WENT UP.

We decided that day to start afresh, to get to know each other again as Vee and Kim in their twenties. To press refresh on the friendship and take it a day at a time. It has now been a year since we re-entered each other's lives and I can safely say, taking that break was the best thing we could've ever done for ourselves, our friendship and our growth. I'm so much more connected to my friend now than ever before. We no longer feel bound to the term 'best friend' as it doesn't define who we are any more. We are incredibly great friends with a deep bond and we are taking each day as it comes. I am ecstatic to have her back in my life and truly enjoy her company, wisdom and love.

What I'm trying to show here is that time, status or position shouldn't keep you bound to anyone or anything. Whether it's your job or a relationship, you should always know that when it's time to move on, take a break or re-evaluate the dynamic, you should do so. Of course, it can be difficult to first admit there's a problem. Often when we love people, we want to hold onto them and see only the good in them. My example with Kim is one of many situations that built up over time. When they went unchecked, they turned into bigger and more unbearable issues. Had we addressed each other earlier on, we could've avoided hurting each other. Speaking up in relationships of all kinds helps to set boundaries; it also helps the other person accommodate you and stop doing things that hurt you. Like I said, if they are intentionally setting out to cause you pain, this is a whole different situation and there is so much help to be found on the internet to assist with emotional and physical abuse. I am referring to the smaller things that may not bother you in isolation, but grouped together can cause a toxic relationship and resentment later down the line.

TIME, STATUS OR POSITION
SHOULDN'T KEEP YOU BOUND
TO ANYONE OR ANYTHING.
WHETHER IT'S YOUR JOB OR A
RELATIONSHIP, YOU SHOULD
ALWAYS KNOW THAT WHEN IT'S
TIME TO MOVE ON, TAKE A BREAK
OR RE-EVALUATE THE DYNAMIC,
YOU SHOULD DO SO.

Learning to check yourself

I used to really struggle with expressing myself. I hated confrontation and hated communicating my feelings. I felt it was a waste of time and that everyone around me should just *know* how to be a good person to me. Looking back, I'm astonished I ever believed life could be such a way. Life is about communication and a big key to empowering yourself is realising your own weaknesses and flaws, and how you contribute to the spaces, energies, and lives of others. My unwillingness to communicate my emotions left the people around me not knowing they were hurting me. Instead, I grew angrier and more distant as they continued to do so. They never understood why, and our relationships suffered because of it.

Confrontation can be healthy sometimes because it helps both people to know where they stand. It helps establish boundaries, and it helps you to learn to be protective of your mental space and happiness.

I got into the habit of better expressing myself after meeting my friend James. He taught me the art of speaking my mind and doing it with conviction. I used to hold back a lot to save the other person's feelings or out of fear of causing tensions. Whenever someone did something to annoy me, I'd bring it up weeks later, instead of telling them on the spot. James questioned why I'd waited so long before making someone aware they had upset me, and I'd mindlessly explain that I needed time to get over the situation before mentioning it. He explained that it was a terrible way to handle things because had I addressed the issue sooner, it would've been solved, or at least acknowledged, sooner. This would tackle the bad habits that were being formed and also avoid tension and conflict building up from both sides. James celebrated me using my voice and that gave me confidence to implement this in my other relationships with those close to me. I now see that confrontation can be healthy sometimes because it helps both people to know where they stand. It helps establish boundaries, and it helps you to learn to be protective of your mental space and happiness. The more you tolerate things you truly hate or find annoying, the more you are burying how you really feel and one day it could become too much. I now actively try and have these tricky conversations with friends and family, because these talks can only help to advance our relationships. The process of expressing myself has now become a lot easier because I know how to manoeuvre in that space, and make these conversations productive and comfortable. My greatest relationships are with the people with whom I can be the most open and honest. They are with the people I can express myself to freely when I'm unhappy about something, which I think is vital for maintaining healthy relationships.

Practical steps to building healthy relationships

1. Acknowledge your feelings. When assessing a difficult relationship with a friend, partner or family member, be sure to actually take some time to sit down and acknowledge the emotions you are feeling. Before you can move on from anything, you must first try and heal or at least process what it is you have just gone through. Knowing where you stand will help when making the difficult and necessary decisions about cutting people off, etc. You need to know where you stand and what you want first.

2. Communicate. Here's a challenge: the next time you feel unhappy about something a friend, partner or family member has done to you, address it. Pull them to one side and have an open conversation about how what they did made you feel. Let them know why you're expressing it to them.

3. Embrace confrontation. I'm not saying be confrontational; it's more that I'm saying don't run away from it. You can have difficult and uncomfortable conversations in a way that allows you to show you're not happy and cannot allow for whatever boundary has been crossed. It's important to show your loved one that you're being serious by not allowing them to brush off your emotions or feelings. Often people brush things off as a joke or a one-off, when in reality, it's something that triggers you and makes you unhappy. Nine times out of ten, people aren't aware they're doing it and this gentle reminder will help them to be more mindful of you and your emotions.

AS ALWAYS, REMEMBER THAT THIS IS *YOUR* LIFE. YOU DO NOT HAVE TO SUBJECT YOURSELF TO STAYING IN TOXIC OR UNCOMFORTABLE RELATIONSHIPS OR BE THE BRUNT OF SOMEONE ELSE'S JOKES *JUST* TO MAKE THEM HAPPY. BE COMFORTABLE WITH BEING UNCOMFORTABLE TO MAINTAIN HEALTHIER, HAPPIER AND MORE EMPOWERED RELATIONSHIPS.

The Importance of Self-Care

MANAGING IT ALL AND STAYING HEALTHY

Another big part of my journey has been learning the art of listening to my body. I read on Twitter once that if you don't choose your rest day, your body will choose it for you.

Recently, there has been a rise in the glorification of hustle culture. The idea that you must always have a manic workload, stay up late and be busy 24/7 to be considered hardworking and successful. This narrative can be found constantly on social media, TV adverts and in movies. Therefore, it's easy to fall into a trap of 1) believing that this is the norm and 2) believing that this is what it takes to get ahead. What most people don't tell you is that in the middle of that 'ten-hour study session', they took a nap. What they won't tell you is that after that ten-hour study session they broke down and cried because they felt stressed, anxious and unhappy. People only show you what they want you to see, so don't beat yourself up if your methods are different to those around you. Stay in your lane, you have nothing to prove to anyone.

Let me give you a simple example of why: I joined a running challenge with my male friends after they dared me to run two kilometres a day for one week. I had never really run before and my legs were not used to it. It took me thirty to forty minutes to complete a two-kilometre run every day and after each one, I was exhausted, but I was determined to show the boys that I could take on any challenge they threw at me. I succeeded and completed the challenge, but this is where things went wrong. They came back and bet me again but this time the stakes were higher. They bet that I couldn't run eighty kilometres in one month and that if I did, I couldn't beat them to the finish line. I, of course, accepted the new mission; the recent victory had clouded my judgement. I now felt like I had something to prove and even the boys wouldn't care if I had declined to participate, I was now determined to win, no matter what.

Now, here is what was wrong with me taking on this new challenge; to begin, I have no idea why I cared to win this challenge, I had no real commitment to running. I was just running because someone had dared me to. So not only was I lacking in interest, I was also lacking in motivation. The only thing that saved me was my ability to repeat the same action every day, no matter how much I disliked it. THAT alone, and my desire to beat the boys, is what helped me slowly clock in my 80 kilometres and beat them to the finish line. Instead of running, as the challenge required, I would take long walks at odd hours and add 15km to my scoreboard while they were distracted with other commitments. I'd come back home with blisters on my feet and my legs aching from lack of stretching. I also became unwell because I was walking during cold nights. None of this mattered to me though because I was determined to put a large distance between me and the boys and beat them as I knew if I waited too long, they would overtake me with their pace. My plan worked and I passed the finish line first without them realising.

Even though I had technically won, in my heart I felt far from a winner. I was mentally deflated and physically my body hurt in places I did not even know could hurt. I had not trained myself to jog or walk long distances like that in such a short space of time. After I had crossed the finish line, I had to stay at home for a week soaking my feet in bath salts to try and bring them back to life and the victory was just not as sweet as I thought it would be. I had thrown myself into a competition with people who were levels ahead of me in the running field. Yes, I had won but only through taking the easy way out, walking not running. Had I have taken part properly, I would not have survived. I had not enjoyed myself and had crossed the finishing line battered and bruised. Had I stopped when I should have, after the 2km a week challenge, I would never gotten the excruciating blisters that my poor feet now had to suffer. I also began hearing talk of a new challenge coming up to run a 100km. I was mortified and realised that the post would keep on moving and I had no desire to try to keep up. I had allowed my eagerness to win overlook the necessity of preparation. Had I prepared better and learned how to stretch, eat clean and preserve my energy, I may have enjoyed myself more. But I didn't and was miserable for it.

IN THIS LIFE, YOU CANNOT ALLOW PEOPLE TO CHALLENGE YOU IN THINGS THAT ARE NOT IN YOUR LANE OR IN YOUR FIELD.

The good thing that came out of the challenge was that I realised how much I had benefited from those long walks. They gave me time and space to think and talk to myself. I realised the fresh air helped me feel more relaxed and that I felt a lot fitter now that I had gotten into regular exercise. The following month I began taking more walks but this time, walking at my own pace, at reasonable hours and for the right reasons. I learned in life, you literally have to run your own race otherwise you end up doing things because you are seeking acceptance and validation. I wanted the boys to see me as one of them and earn their respect. But the thing is, I am not one of them, I am one of me, one of Vee and I have nothing to prove to anyone but myself.

As my friend George always says, you have to take everything one step at a time; something we all learn at a young age but forget to implement when we grow older. You start at ten, you go to twenty, and then you move to thirty. You don't jump levels, you pace yourself and adjust as you go. I no longer feel a pressure to perform or to keep up because my own pace and style are exactly what works for me. If you don't stop and evaluate what you're doing you will become prone to burnout, especially if you try to keep up with other people. We all have different contexts and different starting points. I do my best to focus on my own goals, my own challenges, and try to improve myself to the best of my abilities – not based on someone else's metrics of success.

IF YOU DON'T STOP AND EVALUATE WHAT YOU'RE DOING YOU WILL BECOME PRONE TO BURNOUT, ESPECIALLY IF YOU TRY TO KEEP UP WITH OTHER PEOPLE. WE ALL HAVE DIFFERENT CONTEXTS AND DIFFERENT STARTING POINTS. I DO MY BEST TO FOCUS ON MY OWN GOALS, MY OWN CHALLENGES, AND TRY TO IMPROVE MYSELF TO THE BEST OF MY ABILITIES – NOT BASED ON SOMEONE ELSE'S METRICS OF SUCCESS.

Staying focused

A lot of the time when we lose focus or stop wanting to do things, it's typically because we no longer know why we're doing them. We lose sight of the beginning and the ultimate end. We're just stuck floating along, not knowing which direction we should be swimming in. Implementing the quarterly and pyramid systems for goal setting will help you figure this out, but you still need more. You need to sit down and ask yourself why. *Why do I want to do this?* Be honest with yourself. It's okay if it's simply financially motivated because as we mentioned, 'money makes the world go round'. Being honest about that will help you remember why you're staying late at work or why you're waking up extremely early every morning. Ignoring the true motivation for what you're doing is a mistake that you should try to avoid. For me, I know what my ultimate goals are: to either become the CEO of a global education company or work as the Education Minister in Zimbabwe and the United Kingdom. Everything else happening around me is leading up to those moments. I know it's going to take me many years to get there but, in the meantime, I want to become the change I want to see.

Every day when I wake up, I feel insanely grateful and lucky to be able to do the things that I love. I feel blessed to know what I want to do with my life and follow my purpose. It means that no matter how hard the work gets or how overwhelmed I may become, I can take a step back and clearly see what each sacrifice and each moment is leading up to. If you don't know what your 'thing' is yet, it's okay. I can't stress that enough. It just means that you're on the journey to discovering it and that's equally okay.

I manage to stay on top of my work, my grades, and my social life because I've taught myself how to. I stay on top of my university work because I want to do well but also because I'm ridiculously grateful to be attending an amazing university, learning about the things that I love. Studying International Education Policy has been everything and more. Every day I'm in class, I learn something new that shocks me about girls' education and pushes me to want to do more now and in the future. Another reason why I'm so motivated to succeed is because things could've turned out very differently. Things could've been so much worse. Imagine if I'd stayed in Zimbabwe with the family members who didn't want me? I don't think I would've been as positive as I am today without the support of my mum and sister. Knowing that my life could have been so different makes me even more proud of the one I have now.

In this version of my life, I have the choice to pursue the things I *want* to pursue rather than the things I *have* to. So, when I feel like complaining or giving up, I remind myself that other young girls just like me who are back home don't even get the chance to complain about going to university or about having too many projects on at the same time. When I speak to some of my cousins, my heart breaks into a thousand pieces. They have dreams of pursuing beauty, engineering, becoming teachers or entrepreneurs, but they've been told that they have to get married soon and become stay-at-home mums. When they tell me their stories or those of their friends, I know I have no right to waste my talents or opportunities. I remind myself that there are girls like me, those who literally share the same genes as me, who don't get that chance and would give anything for it.

KNOWING THAT MY LIFE
COULD HAVE BEEN SO
DIFFERENT MAKES ME
EVEN MORE PROUD OF
THE ONE I HAVE NOW.

These thoughts are what make me want to seize life, make change, and help raise our future generation of leaders, the ones who are going to help change the status quo so that girls like my sixteen-year-old cousins can actually bring their dreams to life. I want to live in a world where all girls are given the same chance that boys are, to realise their passions and gain an education. I want to live in a world where students from underrepresented backgrounds can get the support that they need so that we never lose another future leader to the hands of being dismissed or unheard again. I want to live in a world where young people who look like me can look at the media and see positive representations of themselves in spaces that they dream about. I want to live in a world where we don't judge one another based on our differences but rather use them as sources of exchange, embracing each other and learning from one another. I want to live in a world where women are given equal pay for the same work as their male counterparts. I want to live in a world where we can accept each other for who we are, accept people's gender pronouns and stop killing people based on the colour of their skin. I want to live in a world that has love, peace, and acceptance of one another as its core foundations.

How to keep on going

In order to give advice, it's important that I'm transparent about my own processes and how I juggle my own work/life balance. Have you ever heard that saying, 'I can't complain about having too much on my plate if the goal was to eat'? That's my general outlook on life. Many of the things that I'm doing now were once my wildest dreams. They were what I thought only happened to people in movies or people who were 'worthy'. I used to dream of being successful, of being able to give my mother the world and watch her reap the fruits of her labour. I dreamt of attending Oxford and Harvard, of having my own show one day, writing a book and many other things. I used to walk past shop windows and wish I could buy my mum a new fridge because the one at home didn't work properly. I used to dream of being known, of making an impact and having my voice heard. Now, watching my online platform amass over 250,000 human beings who are tuned in to hear what I have to say blows my mind. My biggest wish was to work within the education sector, and now I'm preparing to launch my first EdTech business with my sister. I can't quite believe this is all real life.

How do I do it all? How am I currently writing this book while in the middle of my full-time degree at Harvard? How am I running my online channel as a daily business and preparing the launch? I do it by having the most effective time management system I know of. I look at every single hour as a blessing because I know that once it's gone, it's gone. When I have more to do I tend to focus better because I know how precious my time is and if I don't get it done it'll have to go to the end of the to-do list. I do the things that I love – everything is interconnected and all driven by my passions. This way, I never truly get bored (unless I'm in a class learning how to code education documents).

One of the resources that I use to contribute to my productivity and time management is my Google calendar. It's one of the biggest blessings I've ever had. I can schedule all the details of my life and never forget the commitments I have coming up. I have a terrible memory and know that I have to build a system around me that will help address this. I schedule my friends' birthdays months in advance and remind myself to order gifts. I schedule in monthly self-care days, which are mandatory despite the deadlines or commitments I have that day. I synchronise my personal schedule with my university assignments and deadlines and get an overview of my entire life. Implementing these small changes such as scheduling and using a calendar meant that I was becoming more intentional about my life and how I navigated it. It meant that present Vee could remind future Vee of the things she set out to do and complete. As I mentioned before, the one person I owe the most to is myself, therefore, once I've committed myself to something, I don't enjoy the idea of letting myself down and neither should you. The ability to hold yourself to your own promises is a good one to have. Even if it means adjusting a few things according to context, like living in a pandemic. I promised myself that if I got into Harvard, I would give it my all. I would join all types of societies, make a lot of friends and pass my degree. However, the outbreak of the pandemic meant that things such as joining the cheerleading society, sharing a bedroom with your peers, and celebrating American holidays could no longer happen. It meant that the vision of Harvard that I had promised myself could no longer happen. My ability to adapt depending on the context helped me reframe what was happening and adjust my initial goals.

The work hard, play harder framework

Another thing that helps me stay on top of my work is relaxing and scheduling in days to do nothing but order a takeaway, watch Netflix and sleep. It's impossible to live a life of just work without reward or enjoyment, so whenever I can, I spend quality time with myself to continue discovering who I am. One of my favourite things to do, which I've been doing for a while, is taking myself away. I'm not talking about expensive holidays; I mean mini staycations in England. I always know when I'm about to have a busy season, whether it's my final year exams or having a big project to complete. I plan something at the end of busy seasons. An example of this is during my A-Levels. I knew that after those exams, I'd feel completely exhausted physically and mentally, so I planned to go to the United States for the summer to take part in Camp America. This was something I'd always wanted to do but I knew my mum couldn't take time out of work to come travelling with me as a child. Because of this, the moment I finished my A-Levels – I had finally turned eighteen – I had my airplane ticket waiting for me. Knowing that there was going to be a summer of just fun and relaxation made the moments of sacrifice and revision during my A-levels all the more worth it. I knew that there was a bigger goal at play – getting my education – but we're all human and need something a little more to keep us going.

Where I can, I try to implement a strong 'work hard, play harder' framework. I believe life's too short to only ever work and not actually enjoy what you're doing or what you're creating. When the opportunities arise for me to let my hair down, relax and spend a little on myself, I take it. The way that I see it, for me to be at my best, I need to feel my best. If I'm working 365 out of 365 days, I'm going to be burnt out, bored and one-dimensional.

I FIND THAT WHENEVER I TAKE MY BREAKS EITHER OUT OF THE COUNTRY, OUT OF THE CITY, OR OFF SOCIAL MEDIA, I ALWAYS COME BACK FEELING REFRESHED AND REJUVENATED. IF ANYTHING, TAKING A STEP BACK FROM WORK CAN HELP SPARK NEW IDEAS AND HELP YOU TO INNOVATE MORE THAN YOU THOUGHT.

I find that whenever I take my breaks either out of the country, out of the city, or off social media, I always come back feeling refreshed and rejuvenated. If anything, taking a step back from work can help spark new ideas and help you to innovate more than you thought. This past year I worked incredibly hard. I graduated in July, began my Master's in September and stayed online full-time while also preparing to write this book. It's safe to say it was the busiest time of my life. When December came around, I decided to take a break from social media – a complete blackout, no activity on any of my platforms for two months. Everyone around me said it was impossible. They said it would be damaging, that my audience might become restless and that I wouldn't generate any views or subscribers in the time that I was off. I decided to take the chance anyway and continue with my break. The time off was by far the most refreshing thing I've ever done. During that time, I managed to complete the first draft of my book. I was able to get in tune with my body and my health and began taking my walks again, eating better and becoming more conscious of what I was stocking in my cupboards and fridge.

I learned how to code and took on a voluntary research project about girls' education and donor investments organised by the Centre for Global Development. I really enjoyed taking on this project because it taught me a lot about the field I wanted to go into and imparted a new skill that I never thought I'd acquire. I also began learning about financial literacy, and how to invest my money for long-term gains. I was always hesitant about things like that, but I wanted to lean into my fears and explore things I was running away from. When I began my final semester at Harvard, I felt liberated to choose my classes, and attend and write my assignments, all without sharing it on social media. I couldn't remember the last time I'd done those things without informing my audience. I chose classes

I would've never chosen previously such as a Qualitative Program and Policy Evaluation course just because I wanted to stretch myself and make sure I was able to adapt in unfamiliar situations that could help me build my skill set. I took the time to plan out my year, to think in depth about what I wanted to gain from it, how I wanted to grow, and why I wanted those things.

The time off social media helped me become at one with myself even more than I was before. I was able to do things privately without reading thousands of comments and opinions about it. I hadn't realised how much of what I heard and saw about myself I was internalising, so during that two-month break I took control of how I responded and reacted to what was happening around me. I also took the time to rest, to sleep and to stretch my body. When you're incredibly busy studying or working, you can form habits that you don't notice until later. I could sit at my desk for four to five hours plus without moving, simply because there was so much to do. I neglected taking little breaks and failed to look after myself, ignoring the basic rules of self-care that I learned at the beginning of my journey.

People often think that working hard means putting your body into overdrive, but I'm here to tell you that rest shouldn't be underestimated. Choose a rest day or two and don't let anyone or anything come in the way of that. Try to also implement a strict curfew for when you can no longer work, for example, after 8 pm. Think about what may work for you. Even presidents and prime ministers, famous athletes, and the Beyoncés of the world need sleep, so make sure you don't burn yourself out, or compromise on your sleep or your health.

Don't stop the music

Alongside resting, exercising and taking time off, another thing I find joy in doing and that, in my opinion, makes me really happy and productive is listening to music and dancing. I spend a lot of time alone simply because my mother and sister work away from home which means I need to keep myself busy and occupied. Of course, I study, respond to emails, make videos, etc. but when I have free time, I take my headphones, put them on full blast and play my favourite music and just dance with myself. This is genuinely one of my favourite pastimes and something that lets me release endorphins which in turn makes me happier. I have tried yoga and meditation before but they have never really worked for me. I've realised I do better with constant activity. I like moving and keeping my body active. It allows me to centre my energy, and somehow get focused on tackling the tasks ahead. I sometimes also do my little dance sessions on Instagram with my followers, just as a way of sharing the joy and the type of songs I like.

I believe the kind of music I choose to listen to also plays a huge role in the nature of my mood. I mentioned before that whenever I wanted to be sad about something, I would make sure everything around me was sad, and that included the tunes I absorbed. I would play songs about losing people, getting heartbroken and feeling pain on repeat. The songs would make me cry and my day would feel gloomy, even if it was bright outside. I now use music for the opposite. I use it to make my days better. From the moment that I wake up, I have music playing. My favourite morning song before getting out of bed is 'Hey, Soul Sister' by Train. The beat just makes me want to get up and get going, it makes me feel like the main character in a movie, like I'm living in a music video. I suddenly feel in control of my day and how I want to go about it. Another one of my favourites, slightly more mellow, is 'Brown Skin Girl' by Beyoncé. This song makes me feel nothing but beautiful and empowered in my skin. With songs like this, it's more about the lyrics and the melodies. I feel as though they are speaking to me and reinforcing the positive affirmations in my private journal. These types of songs are constantly blasting in my ears. I hear their positive words repeatedly. I sing and dance along. I allow the energies that were put into creating and releasing these songs to weave around me, and it contributes to my day in a positive and uplifting way. I also love Zimbabwean dance music more than anything in the world. It's one of the most upbeat genres of music that I've ever come across and I feel connected to it through language and my mother tongue. Music is just one of the few things that help me live a life whereby I'm the captain of my own ship.

Practical steps to managing it all

1. Go at your own pace. Remember that you are not running anyone else's race! This is your timing; this is your moment and do not allow others to rush you or push you to go at a speed that is too fast for you.

2. Organise your day and learn to be intentional with your time by using a calendar, a to-do list, a planner, an app, or whatever works for you.

3. Remember to take breaks while you're working and create good habits. It's all well and good working hard, but imagine not being able to enjoy it because you're always exhausted. You have to take time and prioritise breaks so you can recharge and give it your all when you do return to doing the work.

4. Implement a cut-off time for work every day. As well as knowing when to take a break, it is equally important to know when to stop altogether. You must know how to separate work from your relaxation time. In order to have a well harmonised life, you must know when to not overindulge in one activity, i.e. work.

5. Remember to exercise or use your body. Doing so helps you get out of your mind and allows you to think in a totally different way.

6. Take days off for self-care. What do you like to do for fun? How do you like to relax? Whatever your answers are, do it! You deserve to look after yourself and taking time off helps you to recharge. Once you've done this, you can go back to tackling your goals and dreams.

7. Schedule a holiday and reward yourself for a job well done. Whether that be a staycation, somewhere abroad, or time away from social media, it's important to have something pleasurable to look forward to after all your hard work.

Goodbye ...
For Now!

Here we are at the end of our journey together. I have shared all that I can up until this point in my life. I am still studying my Master's degree at Harvard, turning twenty-three in a few months and still very much figuring out this thing called life.

I am making the best of the things around me, the opportunities I've been granted, and will continue to pour my energies into putting good into the world. I hope that when I read this back in a few years, I will be working in a role that makes it possible for girls everywhere to have universal education that is free, safe and good quality. Even if I'm not, I hope that whatever I am doing, I am making myself proud. I hope that you, too, will be doing what you want to do, and will have embarked on a journey of self-empowerment that is helping you discover who you are, what you care about, and how you want to spend your valuable time. I hope you are being kind to yourself and that you're kicking imposter syndrome's butt to the ground.

I CAN'T BEGIN TO TELL YOU HOW EMPOWERING IT WAS WHEN I ACCEPTED MYSELF FOR EVERYTHING I AM, FLAWS AND ALL. SELF-ACCEPTANCE AND SELF-LOVE ARE A ONCE-IN-A-LIFETIME OPPORTUNITY.

Life will become so much easier if you actually *like* yourself because that's one less battle to fight. The first step for me was accepting that my past was the beginning I didn't want but the beginning that I had. So much anger had been bottled up about how I was treated as a child and I had carried it forward with me without realising it. I felt lost in Zimbabwe without my family, and, if I am to speak truthfully, I no longer wanted to live at one point. At my young age, I remember knowing I was unhappy and wondering how I could get to heaven where my dad was. Thinking about those moments now makes me so sad. It makes me want to go back in time and give baby Vee a hug, but I can't, so I've learned how to process the things that happened and use them as my source of strength. I'm now lucky enough to be able to live a life I'm extremely proud of, one that I'm in complete control of and can structure in a way that has the pursuit of happiness and good at its centre. I want the same thing for those of you reading this book, for you to feel like you have some of the tools to go forth and gain control of your life and narrative. I want you to know that you are worthy of love, happiness, and support.

Feeling lost and unsure of what to do next is the worst feeling but it can also be the best because the realisation of those emotions means you're ready for the journey of discovering what comes next. Be prepared to take chances, put yourself out there and ask for help. It's such a sad reality that young people born in less privileged backgrounds have to do twice the work just to end up in the same place as their wealthier peers. It truly angers me, but my anger alone is not going to change anything. We have to use that in order to figure out how to succeed despite these unfair barriers. Learn how to grab the opportunities in front of you, ask for help, seek free resources, make yourself known to your teachers and your peers; those who inhabit the positions that you want. Doing these things – putting yourself out there – will never be comfortable, and I hate that we have to do it, but it's part of the process of getting closer to your goals. If you know someone who works in the role you want (whether offline or online), ask them for some work experience at their workplace, ask to interview them or to introduce you to someone who can help. If you watch someone online whose work you enjoy and find helpful, message them. I have received so many messages online from young people seeking guidance and help and have replied to the ones who were direct about what they needed and how I could help.

I FIND IT FLATTERING WHEN SOMEONE NEEDS MY HELP, SO NEVER BE AFRAID TO ASK. SOME PEOPLE ARE HONOURED THAT YOU FIND THEM INSPIRATIONAL ENOUGH TO WANT GUIDANCE FROM THEM; THEY MIGHT NOT HAVE THE CAPACITY TO HELP YOU, BUT THEY CAN INTRODUCE YOU TO SOMEONE WHO DOES HAVE THE TIME! THIS CAN OPEN DOORS TO MANY DIFFERENT PEOPLE.

Regardless, I hope this book has given you some pointers to where to start as you embark on your journey to living an empowered and happier life, one that puts you at the forefront of your dreams and desires. You might start by looking at your goals and figuring out how to structure them properly, or taking that rejection letter that's been making you sad and reframing it as a source of redirection. Perhaps you'll finally address someone in your life about the pain they've been causing you in order to move towards a healthier relationship or maybe you're more comfortable now with not yet knowing what your purpose is but want to begin the journey of finding out. Whatever it is that you're feeling, I'm glad you've gotten to hear that you're worthy of everything you want to manifest. Remember to stop asking, 'What if I fail?' Rather ask yourself . . . 'What if I fly?'

NOW, GO
TURN THOSE
LEMONS INTO
LEMONADE!

VEE'S READING LIST

Dear Ijeawele, or A Feminist Manifesto in Fifteen Suggestions Chimamanda Ngozi Adichie

The Girl with the Louding Voice Abi Dare

I Am A Girl From Africa Elizabeth Nyamayaro

Why I'm No Longer Talking to White People About Race Reni Eddo-Lodge

Noughts & Crosses Malorie Blackman

Becoming Michelle Obama

Educated Tara Westover

The Hill We Climb Amanda Gorman

I Am Malala Malala Yousafzai

Brit(ish) Afua Hirsch

VEE'S LISTENING LIST

The Michelle Obama Podcast Michelle Obama

To My Sisters Podcast Courtney Daniella & Renee Kapuku

Working Hard, Hardly Working Podcast Grace Beverly

Building You Podcast Hayley Mulenda

Flawless Beyoncé ft. Chimamanda Ngozi Adichie

Moment 4 Life Nicki Minaj ft Drake

Girl on Fire by Alicia Keys ft. Nicki Minaj

Schoolin' Life Beyoncé

Vivir Mi Vida Marc Anthony

thank u, next Ariana Grande

Black Magic Little Mix

VEE'S WATCHING LIST

Hidden Figures

Black Panther

The Hunger Games: Catching Fire

The Queen's Gambit

Grace and Frankie

Acknowledgements

To my wonderful best friends, Malala Yousafzai and Josh Tulloch: Thank you for your encouragement, your unwavering support and your ruthless feedback in the process of creating this book. Dear Malala, since the birth of this idea you have stood by my side as I have stressed, stayed up late at night doing proofreads and going through endless subtitle ideas until we found the one. I have confided in you endlessly about my thoughts, and every time you held them with care, thought and delicate consideration. You helped me reignite my light when I hit writer's block, and now you help me celebrate the art that is now this book, and I want to thank you for that.

Josh, my dear best friend, you have never dismissed any of the ideas I share with you, and I will never forget the first time I mentioned this book to you and how encouraging and excited you were as if it was already written. You were one of the first people I wanted to call once I had said yes to Penguin, and for me, that speaks volumes. I am positive there are times when you believe in me more than I believe in myself. Your unapologetic support, guidance and love mean the world to me. You have helped me to see this book in a brighter light than I could ever have imagined, and have played a considerable role as my source of inspiration for the words I have woven into this book, and for that, amongst many other things, I am forever grateful.

To my incredible editor Mireille Harper, thank you for seeing the vision of this book long before we ever met. From the first email you sent describing the idea of a book I already had in mind, I knew we were in sync and drawing from the same energy sources. I loved how you saw me correctly and understood what I stood for and cared about without me having to explain. Your ability to encourage and give constructive criticism is impressive. You have made me feel comfortable, seen and valued throughout this whole process.

I have never doubted your support, and your sensitivity while handling personal stories and anecdotes of my life has been refreshing. From the moment I handed my manuscript over to you and your team, I have been nothing but secure and excited to bring this out to the world. To Jennifer Obidike, thank you for your kind, careful and sensitive edit notes, you were terrific to work with because of your patience and understanding nature. And to Maxine Sibihwana for always sharing your excitement for this book and reminding me why I began writing it in the first place. I am also grateful to the entire team at Square Peg and VINTAGE, who have poured love and support into this project; it means the world to me.

I owe a lot of my gratitude to my close friends who have helped me with regular proofreading, and have trusted me with their stories and experiences and allowed me to share them with the world. I am incredibly grateful to my longtime friend and now sister, Kimberley Coupe. Kim, your support and constant loyalty has helped me grow into the woman I am today. Thank you for letting me openly share our friendship and some of the struggles we endured and how we have managed to maintain our 17-year friendship. You hold a special place in my heart, and I can't wait for us to grow old together.

I also want to thank my other amazing friends who have served as my motivation and inspiration while writing this book because, without your incredible contributions to the world, I would not have provided so many empowering examples for other young people throughout this book. I also owe many thanks to my high school History teacher, Mr James Ball. You are a phenomenal teacher, and from you, I learned what it means to truly mentor young people with grace and love. Your leadership style and ability to make your students feel seen, heard and valued is groundbreaking, and your lasting effect on my confidence is a testament to that. Thank you for always encouraging me to dream bigger than I was initially and teaching me to always use my voice and stand up for what I believe in no matter what. Your unwavering guidance and support in my school years have been a catalyst to my self-empowerment journey, and for that, I am forever indebted to you.

Most of all, I would like to thank my incredible family, for whom I would not be where I am today without. Firstly, my wonderful mother, Loveness Kativhu, the person to whom this book is dedicated. I do not think I could ever articulate in words just how much you mean to me and how your journey through life is one of the things that motivates me every single day. Knowing how much you have had to sacrifice, give up and lose just to give my sister and me a chance at life pushes me to work hard and pursue all of my dreams. You have shown that you can defy the odds and not allow the negative that happens to you to define you or dictate your path. Your endless love has made me the fearless, strong and loving young woman I am today. Your support goes beyond that of human capability, and knowing you support me 100 per cent no matter what gives me the confidence I need to walk tall and proud in whatever I do. I love you dearly, and I hope you love this book and that the words I have written about you finally help you see just how incredible a mother you are.

Finally, I would like to end by thanking my life partner and my soul mate, my sister, Fadzai Kativhu. You are one of the best things that life has given me; having an older sister like you is more than I could have dreamed of. I love the relationship that we have and that we are best friends before anything else. I love that you are constantly fighting my corner and celebrating my achievements like they are your own. You have helped me write this book by staying up with me while I finish drafts, going through the intricate details of our childhood to help me remember the many memories we have shared. You have served as my sounding board and the person I can confide in for this process's excellent and challenging moments. I love doing life with you and feel very lucky to have you as an example to follow as I grow up. You are the best big sister a girl could ask for, and I love you dearly. We did it together, and now we get to share our life with the world! You and mom have made it possible for me to become the woman I am today and now the author that those who read *Empowered* get to see. I wish our father, Brighton Kativhu, was still here to share this moment with us, but I know that he is in heaven beaming with pride, and in that, I find comfort and peace.